THE KEY TO SUCCESS, LOVE, FRIENDSHIP, AND YOUR CAREER IS *RIGHT AT YOUR FINGERTIPS*

Here, at last, is a book that simply and lucidly teaches you the extraordinary science of Graphology. With clear, step-by-step directions, Robert Holder's new easy method of handwriting analysis enables you—in virtually no time at all—to make accurate character evaluations, uncover hidden personality traits, and even foretell future actions.

Whether you're simply curious or purely practical, the dozens of illustrations, detailed personality descriptions, Grapho-guides, and valuable tips included provide you with all the information necessary for starting a fascinating hobby which can lead to a highly profitable career.

You Can Analyze Handwriting

A Practical Tool for Self-Knowledge
and Personal Power

by Robert Holder

A SIGNET BOOK

NEW AMERICAN LIBRARY

Dedicated to my wife,
Betty Curzon, and our three V's...
Vivian, Victoria, and Valerie

Preface

Your handwriting is a picture of yourself that you may never have seen. This book shows you how to look at handwriting to discover personality and character differences and then apply psychological knowledge to profit from this new information. Graphology is the science of finding out about a person's character from his handwriting. Combine this with psychology and you have the theme of this volume: *Psychographology*.

Because handwriting is a universal means of communication and expression, it is the basis of finding important personality information, not only about yourself but about other people that you are interested in.

The book is organized simply so that you can read it quickly. Illustrations are located immediately following the text discussions so that you will understand promptly just what is being described. Instead of following a straight format, the various sections of the book have been styled to accommodate the sense of the material.

This is not a book to read and set aside. It contains a complete section on Graphology so that it can be used as a continuous reference work on handwriting analysis. This basic material will have to be read many times before it will be mastered.

There is also a list of personality "types" so that you can classify people quickly when you have only a little time to study their handwriting.

A special group of "Grapho-Guides" has been included for the person who cannot wait to finish the book but who needs to try out his new handwriting knowledge immediately. These will serve to answer a number of the most common questions that people want answered about themselves and others.

Proceed cautiously with this new information. Do not make the mistake of thinking that the mere reading of this book and the memorizing of its principles will turn you into a better person. Whether or not you will benefit personally depends on how you use this information. Intelligent effort will point you in the right direction and help you foil failure.

If you stay with Psychographology, increasing your psychological knowledge along with your handwriting analysis facts, you should enjoy a richness of experience that will surprise and please you.

R. H.

Acknowledgments

● **A Note of Thanks to:**

Buffalo State Hospital, Department of Mental Hygiene, State of New York, for help in the procuring of handwriting specimens of mentally ill individuals.

Marvin A. Block, M.D., Buffalo, New York, Chairman, Committee on Alcoholism, American Medical Association, Council on Mental Health, for his cooperation in securing the handwriting of persons under treatment for alcoholism.

Harry J. Anslinger, Commissioner, United States Bureau of Narcotics, for making it possible to secure handwriting specimens of drug addicts.

Dr. M. F. Ashley Montagu, author of *The Natural Superiority of Women*, for so graciously consenting to let me reproduce a specimen of his writing and to print a handwriting analysis based upon his script.

Mr. Louis Hausman, Vice President of CBS Radio, for the use of portions of his handwriting.

Joseph J. Sconzo, M.D., Director, Buffalo State Hospital, Department of Mental Hygiene, State of New York, for help in the procuring of handwriting specimens of mentally ill individuals.

. . . and to the thousands of nameless individuals who have had their handwriting scrutinized by me in my search for new knowledge about the mysteries of human personality prediction.

CONTENTS

Part 1

YOU ARE WHAT YOU WRITE

Part 2

THE WAY YOU WRITE AND WHAT IT MEANS

Part 4

MAKING USE OF THE OPPORTUNITIES THAT HANDWRITING KNOWLEDGE OFFERS YOU

13. Determining your own personality qualifications through handwriting (Cont'd)

Part 1

You are what you write

1. What a knowledge of handwriting can do for you

Do You Really Know Yourself? Did You Know That *Handwriting* Mirrors Character? Would You Like To Learn How To See People As They Really Are?

A knowledge of what your handwriting means may change your life

Every time you write your name you are registering a pen picture of your personality. If you could set down your signatures in a continuous line, from your first schoolboyish scribble to that stylized autograph of yours, you would have a portrait in writing of your character from childhood to adulthood.

The story of the development of your character from year to year would be seen in the script, just as a slice of a log tells in the concentric rings how the weather helped or retarded the growth of the tree.

But you are not felled timber. You are very much alive and growing. You have many chances to adjust your mental and physical environment so that you will grow straight and develop normally.

Handwriting reveals your present and past growth

Your handwriting will reveal the nature of your present and past growth. If it satisfies you, the next step is to study the writing of others so you may understand what is happening in their lives.

If you are not satisfied, you will want to see yourself the way your handwriting mirrors you so that you will have a true picture of your personality.

Know yourself first—then know others—then enjoy the

thrill of fitting in with the whole human family because you will understand people.

You will never again have that feeling of being alone

When you start to read character from handwriting (the science of Graphology), you will discover that many people fall into general personality types, of which you might possibly be one. You will also find out that, regardless of financial or social success, even the leaders in the community and the nation have their weaknesses. You will have revealed to you, also, what traits of character helped them to achieve success.

You will discard that cheerless untruth that there is no one else in the world like you. You will find out that there is no one *quite* like you, but that you have millions of general counterparts everywhere in the world.

If you amazingly turn up handwriting evidence to prove you are a genius, just remember the genius is a *type,* too. We have had them before and expect to keep having them.

You are what you write—but you don't have to stay that way

When you look at your handwriting and classify yourself as a particular type of personality or as a complex bundle of entangled human nature you do not have to stay the way you see yourself. This book will reveal how you can change for the better and find life stimulating.

Why your handwriting reveals the real you

You are not what you think you are, nor are you what other people imagine you to be. You tend to forget your faults, and you magnify your good points. Six different people will see you six different ways.

Your handwriting will record an accurate picture of the *real* you because it is the end result of your brain in action. When you write, you think. To prove this, try to write an intelligent statement without keeping your mind on what you are writing. You will find it will be impossible. Your brain must tell your hand just how to write the words that you "see" in your mind. Your nervous system acts as the "wires" along which the messages of how to write will travel. Hence, stimulated by the brain, your muscular system is coordinated into a more or less controlled writing movement.

The handwriting that evolves is as personal as your finger-prints. Pressure, size, slant, style, letter shapes, spacing, and scores of other details of writing can and do vary in every-body's script. Your writing will also change according to the mood of the moment, a change, however, which will not affect your basic writing movements.

Children write like children. Adults write like adults

When you were a child you wrote like a child. Your hand-writing was large and slowly formed, it was awkward and lacked rhythm, and it reflected the immaturity and simplicity of your childhood. You wrote like this:

you see is news

But when you grew up you put away childish things. You wrote like the complex person into which you had matured. Your writing was no longer simple. It mirrored the character traits and the personality twists which you had acquired. The simple ingredients of childhood had become the infinitely complex blend of millions of experiences which are now com-positely recognized as *you*. And you write accordingly.

No two persons write the same way

That is why no two persons write exactly the same way. They couldn't even if they wanted to. Our whole system of credit would collapse if one person's signature were not singularly different from that of another.

The nearer you are to your early childhood, the more your writing will resemble a child's. The farther you have advanced to maturity, or in establishing yourself as an individual, the more your script will reveal how grown up you are. Here is a sample of the writing of a person who has matured:

I believe this is what you need for. info' —

A bright new world can be yours

This book will show you how to use handwriting study to pick out personality and character clues and then how to apply many of the findings of modern psychology to help open up a bright, new world for you, for your family, for your friends, and for any other people who might interest you.

Graphology will be easy for you if you add this new information to what you already know about people. The behavior of those in your immediate family and that of close friends is bound to be fairly clear to you. Build upon this knowledge, using handwriting analysis as the master key to unlock personality mysteries.

Psychographology is the layman's answer to personality problems

In these pages you will find out about the new and highly useful science called Psychographology, which adds modern psychographological principles to the science of Graphology. You can actually "do-it-yourself" by merely looking at your own and other's handwriting.

Handwriting is your raw material. This book is your power tool

Using this book as a tool, with as much handwriting as you wish to work on, and employing a full set of psychological "attachments," you will be able to understand people who have puzzled you for years, as well as find out all about yourself. This method of objective self-inspection will remove any blinds spots you may have in your personality since you will not be able reasonably to dispute the scientific findings covered in the section on Graphology. You will admit any weaknesses in your character and will want to do something about them.

You will also know your strengths and can build upon them for more satisfaction and profit.

Know yourself by using handwriting clues

Before you can improve your character, refine your personality, smooth your relations with others, advance in your job or succeed in business, attain happiness in marriage, get rid of unhealthy practices or attitudes, or free yourself from silly or sickening fears and frustrations, you must get a clear, personal picture. You must know yourself.

That is the first step, and handwriting analysis will make that initial pace positive and reassuring. Self-knowledge will give you confidence that you know what you are doing and that what you are doing is right. You will respect yourself for what excellent talents you will undoubtedly discover. Other people will catch the contagion of glowing self-esteem and reflect it in your direction. The doors to many situations will begin to open almost before you touch the knobs.

Maybe you are an engineer who secretly loves to sing, but fear of making a fool of yourself has prevented you from joining a choral group. When you find out from looking at your handwriting that you have a wonderful sense of rhythm and musical sensitivity, your fear will vanish and you will add a new happiness to your life.

Perhaps you are a banker who would be advanced into a public relations vice-presidency but you lack facility in talking before groups. A glance at your writing discloses that you have excellent spatial relation knowledge, that you have word fluency, that you have a sparkling sense of humor—but that you also have inordinate personal pride. The latter prevented you from taking a course in public speaking at the local Adult Education center. Now that you know what held you back, that you were just blind to an important personal improvement because you thought it was beneath your dignity to "go back to school," you will drop the deadweight and advance unhampered.

You can also soft-pedal that which you cannot prevent in your personality, you can concentrate on constructive elements of your character, you can relate your interests and your vocational aptitudes to your present job and your future job advancement, you can use your new knowledge gleaned from handwriting study to solve every possible personal problem so that the solution fits the *real you*, as you now will know yourself.

Handwriting knowledge will show you how to get along with other people

Why is it that you find it difficult to adjust to certain persons? Is it because you can't get along with people in general? Or is it because *nobody* can get along with these people? Wouldn't it be helpful to know for certain which fact is true? Think of the peace of mind that would be yours if you found out that it was the other person's fault that your human relations were snarled and unpleasant. Then imagine how good you would feel if you could help that other individual to unsnarl his tangled-up character. It would be highly worthwhile if that other person were your wife, a business associate, a neighborhood child or your own child, a fellow-worker, or the new member of the Board of Directors who came into your group via the purchase of a big block of common stock.

There are many places in life where you must get along with people. You have no other choice. Handwriting will solve this perennial problem.

Graphology is something you can study anywhere in the world at any hour of the day. Wherever there is writing or whenever you observe people penning a piece of script you will be able to discover new information about human beings. What study or science could be easier?

You won't learn everything overnight, but you won't need to. After only a few trials you will be amazed at what you will be able to tell from a mere glance at a specimen of handwriting. Each new analysis will increase your skill.

Fitting into the right job is made easier through handwriting analysis

All sorts of special talents and aptitudes are quickly seen in handwriting. Musical ability, scientific bent, dramatic feelings, mathematical skill, constructive and designing talent, artistic leanings, a natural selling sense, leadership traits, aptitude for research, a genius for working with others, promotion and merchandising senses are only a few of the job suggesters that show in handwriting.

You have only to look at your handwriting to see if you are in the right job. The right job will be the one that coincides with your interests and aptitudes. It may not be the one that pays you the most money. It will be the position that leaves you in a general state of happiness rather than depressing you daily by its deadening drudgery.

Since it is only natural to be dissatisfied and to aim constantly for self-improvement, do not make the easy mistake of thinking you are a vocational misfit simply because you are not getting the most out of your lifework. You may not be putting the most into your job. You may be marking time looking for something better when you have the best chance for success and happiness in your present position. Study your handwriting to see if you are using hidden talents. Maybe a shift to another department in the same organization would result in doubling your salary.

Every once in a while a clerk realizes that he is wasting his talents as a natural-born salesman by slaving away at an inside selling job. He takes a job requiring travel, opening up new vistas of enjoyment and profit for him. Perhaps a look at your handwriting will inspire you to make this move.

Marriage happiness can be helped by using handwriting

Whether you are in the process of picking a marriage partner or whether you are already married, you will find it revealing to know more about the other person. Single individuals can avoid the shock of marrying an abnormal person. They can also select a partner with whom they would be compatible. Ideals can be matched, preferences can be considered, and physical characteristics can be checked in advance. What a man wants in a wife and what a girl desires in a husband are all plainly pictured in handwriting. You can minimize the chance of your marriage ending up in divorce if you take a little care in thinking over the characteristics displayed in your proposed partner's handwriting before you make the final decision.

Family peace can be possible by calming down the aggressors

If your household is in constant turmoil and upset due to the clashes and conflicts of different personalities, don't think that this tenseness has to continue. A study of the handwriting of the various members of your family may reveal that one or more people in the group are over-aggressive, extra-antagonistic, or supersensitive in their attitudes. Talking thing over in a "family council" type of group therapy may easily eliminate much unnecessary bickering, baiting, and downright negation.

Knowledge is power, and power can spell peace. Everybody wants to be peaceful, but they must first learn how.

You will be able to understand children by examining their writing

If you are a parent or a teacher, you can use handwriting analysis to help understand children. Whether or not you help them with your new knowledge, you will get along with them better. Children know when you understand them and will cooperate more readily.

As a parent you will be interested in watching the physical, mental, and emotional progress of your child so that you can step in at the proper moments to provide the guidance and direction that only you as a parent can give. School work, friends of the opposite sex, possible vocational choices, and many other parent-child problems can be diagnosed and solved if a close study of the young person's handwriting is made.

A teacher can use handwriting knowledge to distinguish between the lazy student and the retarded learner, to note important changes in adolescent growth which would have to be considered in teaching that particular child, to spot the real juvenile delinquent, to "understand" some of the "foolish" things that school age children do, and to note the bright pupils early so that assignments might be geared to fit their precocious talent.

Businessmen can improve business relations and human relations

If you are in business you will be interested immediately in how to detect an honest worker. The handwriting of prospective employees will reveal their reliability. Businessmen are notoriously poor judges of character; it may be because they see so many people at close range that they get confused. Everybody looks like everybody else.

Public relations is another concern of the businessman. If he fails in this important activity, his business fails along with it. A study of your handwriting may convince you that, if you do not have the proper promotional kind of personality, it might pay you to step into the background and have some other person take care of meeting the public.

If you are the "boss" and several hundred people depend upon your "mood" for their working happiness, you could decide to stabilize your personality and thus bring equanimity where before there was uncertainty. Then, too, you may have a "depresser" in your organization who makes your moodiness seem all the worse. You might get rid of him. As "boss" you have access to everybody's handwriting. It would pay you to take a look "behind the scenes."

Handwriting will warn you of unhealthy practices and attitudes

We all have our own ideas about what is good for us and what will harm us. Maybe we don't believe that working too hard and too fast hurts us. We may smoke, drink, over-eat, lose sleep, indulge in physical excesses, and the like because we don't think other people can tell us how they harm us personally. But your handwriting will mirror you just as you are at the moment you write. It is almost like going to a doctor and having him hand you a chart giving the graphic story of your health.

If you will look at your handwriting you will see if your way of life is affecting your mental or physical health. Dissipation will show, deterioration will reveal itself, change will be immediately apparent, fear will drag itself through your writing, frustration will grip your script, and the approach of a nervous breakdown will be noted so that you can stop it before it happens.

One unsocial attitude, a single negative tangent in your living, or just too much insistence may block you from great personal success and happiness. You will believe it if you, yourself, observe it in your writing and you will undoubtedly desire to do something about changing the particular phase of your personality that is wrong.

Take this book as a *hand* tool, if you must, and chisel away your rough spots.

Free yourself from harmful fears through handwriting knowledge

Everybody is afraid of something, but nobody should be afraid of everything. Some people are always in a state of anxiety or worry. Your handwriting will tell you just how fearful you are, what situations cause you fright, whether the fears are temporary or permanent, and if you use the psychographological suggestions contained in this book, you will be able to erase the fears that make you miserable.

After all, how can you be afraid of something that you know all about and understand?

Stand in the dark in a strange room. Let your imagination run riot. If something touched you lightly on the top of the head, something that you did not expect, and then there was the sudden crashing of broken glass, you might possibly stand unperturbed! You also might not. Then if the lights went on and you heard the voice of someone you knew saying: "Oh, the wind must have blown the loose pane out of that window and broken it," and you looked up and noted a swinging light cord above your head, you would lose all your unfounded fears!

It is normal to fear the unknown, but knowledge is power.

How certain people can profit from handwriting revelations

A salesman can avoid irritating a prospective customer by knowing ahead of time that person's dislikes.

A banker can keep his bank clear of dishonest people—except bank robbers.

A probation officer can receive indication of just how far he will be able to trust his charges.

A judge will be able to corroborate his wise judgments of the truth of witnesses' testimony.

A lawyer will be able to size up new clients who come to him for legal advice.

A purchasing agent will be able to know just how much of a salesman's story to believe.

A social worker will be able to get closer to his people because he will be able to see behind cold facts or statistics.

A personnel manager will save himself *years* of useless interviewing by quick general employee screening through handwriting study.

A politician will be able to know who his real friends are.

A principal will be able to pick the best possible teachers for his school.

A Board of Education can weed out undesirables in the whole school personnel set-up.

A supervisor could select employees likely to succeed as foremen.

A chain store organization could pick their managers according to a desired chain store manager pattern.

A TV manufacturer could select people who would be able to handle detailed assembly work on TV sets.

A department store could save time and money by not hiring clerks who could not be taught to get along with customers.

A credit service could limit credit to business persons who showed too many speculative tendencies.

A wealthy person hiring domestics could know quickly the type of individuals he was employing.

A college registrar could select the "best" when the qualifications of prospective students seemed practically equal, thus assuring the "cream of the crop" for his college.

FIFTY QUESTIONS WHICH CAN BE ANSWERED FROM A LOOK AT YOUR OWN HANDWRITING

1. Am I dependable?
2. Do I need companionship?
3. Am I 100 per cent honest?
4. Am I affectionate?
5. Can I take responsibility?
6. Do I have executive ability?
7. Do I irritate people?
8. Do I talk too little?
9. Do I talk too much?
10. Do I have the kind of personality that people like?
11. What are my faults?
12. Am I in good health?
13. Am I too energetic?
14. Am I broadminded?
15. Am I careless?
16. Do I have high ideals?
17. Would I succeed in business?
18. Do I have artistic talent?
19. Do I have musical ability?
20. Do I have mechanical ability?
21. Do I have a scientific mind?
22. Am I a logical thinker?
23. Do I control my emotions?
24. Am I too dignified?
25. Do I think too much of myself?
26. Am I the home-loving type?
27. Do I like children?
28. Am I too practical?
29. Am I selfish?
30. Am I generous?
31. Am I extravagant?
32. Am I too sensitive?
33. Do I have a sarcastic tongue?
34. Can I save money easily?
35. Do I take many chances?
36. Do I often put personal pleasure before duty?
37. Do I treat people with tact?
38. Am I sincere?
39. Do I make a good first impression?
40. What type of person should I marry?
41. Would I make a successful salesman?
42. Do I have imagination and insight?
43. Am I very friendly?
44. Do I have much moral courage?
45. How may I improve my personality?
46. Do I appreciate culture?
47. Do I keep my promises?
48. Do I like people?
49. Do I have an understanding nature?
50. Am I normal?

Graphology at a Glance

The following list gives you a speedy over-all view of just what handwriting analysis covers. Select the item on the right that interests you and then turn to the section on Graphology to get the details.

Add what you have learned about modern psychology to this foundation material of handwriting analysis and you will be able to find out about yourself and others immediately. Read the entire book if you need a refresher course in applied psychology.

The basic facts of Graphology can be understood regardless of what your background of learning is. You simply have to be able to tell how one sample of handwriting differs from another. It is in those differences that the whole science of handwriting lies.

Handwriting Characteristics	Personality Characteristics
Spacing of writing	State of mind
Speed of writing	Amount of energy
Slope of writing	Degree of affections
Size of writing	Concentrative powers
Line of writing	State of disposition
Terminal strokes	Degree of generosity
Capital letters	Personal tastes
Small letters	Mental development
Signature	Individuality
Flourishes	Superficialities
Style	Sharpness of mind
Margins	Sense of proportion
Pressure	Emotional state

Learn to use Graphology by trying it out a little at a time until you are sure you understand how it works. You will be surprised how successful you will be after even a small amount of practice. Dealing with the details will automatically give you the confidence to complete a full-scale analysis.

Remember, after a bricklayer has mastered the skill of laying bricks—one brick at a time—there is no limit to the number of bricks he can lay.

Graphology has the same unlimited possibilities once the art of analysis has been achieved.

2. How to get started analyzing handwriting

How to select a proper handwriting specimen

For a quick picture of an individual's personality all you need is any scrap of his handwriting. It can be in pen or pencil. It can be a signature on the back of a check, a hastily written inter-office memo, or the list of groceries on a shopping list. What you will be able to find out, however, will be limited by the kind and the number of your handwriting samples.

The 10 rules for analyzing handwriting

To make a scientific analysis of a person's writing you should follow these simple rules:

1. Do not use a single sample of writing, but use two or three samples, and perferably these should be written a few months apart.

2. Use handwriting written in ink, if possible.

3. Do not use writing which was especially penned to be analyzed.

4. Do not use addresses written on envelopes since the writing will not be natural. Extra muscular control is generally exercised to make the writing clear and legible so the letter does not go astray.

5. Use handwriting written on unlined paper so that base lines will follow the writer's style and spacing will fit the intent of the person writing.

6. Each handwriting specimen should be long enough to contain all the letters of the alphabet, a good assortment of capitals, enough lines of writing to judge spacing and style, and plenty of t-crossings and i-dots to establish supporting evidence in one direction or another.

7. Use handwriting which is as recent as possible.

8. Do not look for certain signs in writing to back up what you "know" about an individual. What you "know" may not be correct. The handwriting will reveal the truth.

9. When you are doing a spur-of-the-moment analysis of someone's writing, ask the person to do the following:

    (a) Write his full name.

    (b) Write a sentence about the weather, such as: "It is very warm out today."

    (c) Write something personal, such as: "I like to play golf."

    (d) Write the alphabet in capital letters.

    (e) List the numbers from one through ten.

10. Under no circumstances pay any attention to what people say about themselves when they are being analyzed, nor try to work the context of any written material into your analysis. Complete objectivity is necessary for an accurate analysis.

Make a record

After you have selected an adequate handwriting sample, check it for the details printed on the Graphological Record blank (*see* page 33) and record your findings on the sheet. This will force you to examine the writing for all the important features of the script which otherwise you might overlook, especially when you make your first few handwriting studies.

In the "Special Feature" part of the blank where there is a space after each capital letter, use the space only where you find significantly different capital letters, and then draw a facsimile of the capital letter for later interpretation.

The purpose of the Graphological Record blank is to systematize your handwriting analysis. It provides you with a permanent record for quick reference or comparison at a later date, should you make another analysis of the same person. Also, if you make enough records of the same handwriting over a period of years you will build up a chronological handwriting history of the person analyzed.

The Record blank will also make it simpler for you to refer to the Personality Type section since you will have a summary of the handwriting features before you for ready use. They can be checked off as you try certain signs for possible type classification.

Your next job is to find out what the various graphological signs mean and then write them down on a sheet of paper as you discover them. When you see that two or more details of the writing suggest the same personality or character trait, add a check after the characteristic concerned, keeping in mind that each check is that much more supporting evidence of the existence of that trait in the individual under study.

Now compare the script with the "Grapho-Guides" to obtain a general personality picture, noting the information on the analysis sheet. The "Grapho-Guides" will be found in a separate section at the conclusion of this chapter.

No.........

GRAPHOLOGICAL RECORD

of...

Address..   City ... . State.....   ....

date.......................................

GENERAL FEATURES:

Margins: wide ......narrow .... medium ....smaller towards bottom.......larger ....

Spacing: (between lines), regular.......irregular.......large.......small ....

Angle of inclination: vertical......left 60°......45°......right 60°.......45°...... 30°.......... ..

Rhythm: long, swinging.......short, choppy.......extremely broken rhythm ....

Legibility: small, legible.......medium, legible.......well-formed letters ....

Illegibility: disorderly.......very plain letters ....

Basic line: straight.......up.......down.......irregular.......word drops at end....... ....

Pressure: heavy ....light.......medium.......uneven.......muddy....... Notes: ....

Rounded writing: small .letters.......? capitals.......? Note ....

Angular writing: small.......large, irregular.......printed .... squeezed ....

Signature: same as body.......larger.......underscored.......enclosed ....flourish ....

NOTES: ....

SPECIAL FEATURES:

Small letters: large.......small.......angular.......rounded ....pressure ....

NOTES: ....

Capitals A.......B.......C.......D.......E.......F.......G.......H.......I.......J....   K...

L.......M.......N.......O.......P.......Q.......R.......S.......T.......U.......V....

W.......X.......Y....... Z......................

NOTES: ....: ....

Strokes:

Beginning: none ....long.......very short...........................

Ending: none.......upward curl.......downward slash ....long.......short ....

Connecting: broken ....long.......short.......variable ....

Hooks: up.......down.......heavy.......ordinary.......Notes ....

Loops:

above basic line: high ....short.......low.......rounded.......inflated ....

below basic line: long.......no return..·.....mere stroke ....inflated ....

REMARKS:

Set yourself straight on these important points

Before proceeding any further it would be wise to set yourself straight on some general misconceptions concerning handwriting analysis as well as provide you with some special and very necessary graphological and psychological information. Some people are so involved with the writing movement when they write that they subconsciously picture themselves as they write. They will draw a subtle picture of their physical appearance. Tallness, shortness, and either an over-weight or under-weight condition are often set down in script.

Very tall people write small letters which are very tall.

Short, stocky people will fashion their small letters shorter than usual.

Persons of average weight will write a medium-pressured script.

Over-weight people will write a heavy-pressured signature.

Under-weight persons will write a light-pressured signature.

There's no such thing as "poor" or "good" writing

When you are analyzing handwriting, remember that there is no such thing as "poor" writing and "good" writing. The more that a handwriting departs from the plain letter-forms learned in school, the more does it indicate the individuality of the writer. Since individuality may be good or bad, the writing is neither one nor the other. There are "smart" criminals and "stupid" citizens, as well as the usual kind in each group.

Determining the sex of the writer

You cannot be absolutely certain of the sex of a writer since most people are blends of masculinity and femininity, and will write according to their individual combinations. However, female writing will be prettier to look at, more rhythmic and decorative, as well as penned with a lighter pressure than that of a male. The masculine writer will write plainly, use a heavy pressure, and will shade his letter strokes. His t-crossings will generally be firm, full-pressured, and long. Hooks, underlines, and periodic places where pressure is increased are some other signs of masculinity.

How to tell the age of the writer

Age in handwriting cannot be determined with certainty, but it can often be arrived at by a comparative analysis using rhythm, pressure, maturity of letter formations, and spacing. Poor rhythm means either a young person or a very old person. Simple letter styles suggest youth; involved or flourished letters point to a person at least over 21. Light pressure, if continuous and rhythmic, suggests a young individual. A light but broken pressure indicates a middle-aged person or older.

Health factors revealed in writing

Your state of health will affect your handwriting. If you are in good health your writing will be smooth and rhythmic. There will be no interrupted strokes. Poor health will disturb your usual way of writing.

If you write with a light pressure you will be most susceptible to eye trouble, heart disease, and tuberculosis. Heavy-pressured writers will be most susceptible to diseases of the bowels and kidneys.

Near-sighted people will always begin a line of writing so that it slants at a different angle from the one preceding it. In addition, the line of writing will be uneven.

Deficiencies in a person's breathing organs are shown in handwriting by the presence of rifts or catches in the loops and curves above the line. Heart trouble is evidenced by breaks in the writing, especially in the tops of the small l's and h's.

Abdominal diseases are displayed in the script of a person who makes his small p and g with crippled lower portions.

Spotting the abnormal person

You will have little trouble in picking out the abnormal individual from his handwriting. The writing will appear abnormal. Generally speaking, the writing will be extreme in one way or another. Large writing will become extra-large, small writing will be almost microscopic; pressure will be muddy, heavy, and crude, or so light the pen barely marks the paper; capital letters will be almost single strokes or they will be surrounded with onion-ring circles or ornate flourishes. Underlines will be repeated by numerous underscores beneath a signature, lines of writing will run into each other in a wild, uncontrolled entanglement, and all the other normal ways of writing will be either magnified or almost neglected. The kind and degree of abnormality will determine the way the writing will reveal it.

Differences caused by types of writing instruments

In making an analysis you should make note of the limitations embodied in the use of different kinds of writing instruments. Pencil writing will not reveal pressure properly. Steel pen script will show stroke shading which may not be typical of the regular writing. A cheap fountain pen may suggest disturbances in rhythm when actually the writer had difficulty in keeping the ink flowing easily. A ball point pen will falsely show heavy pressure, even with light-pressured writers. Hence, before making an analysis you should find out what type of writing device was used.

Using the GRAPHO-GUIDES

The purpose of the "Grapho-Guides" is to make it possible for you to get a quick look at the personality of the writer in question. Once you are familiar with them you will realize their chief usefulness and their apparent limitations. Run your handwriting sample through the complete set for an over-all character pattern.

Have fun with handwriting

Don't worry about what you find out, either about yourself or others. Decide to be happy and constructive in your approach to this new fund of psychological knowledge. If you find deficiencies in your own character, the next step is to act in such a way that they will be corrected in due time. What you come across in other people's personalities in the way of faults can be noted with the possibility of your helping them, at least by a visible attitude of understanding.

Further on in this book you will find opportunities to classify yourself and others into personality types.

There is also a section dealing entirely with the plain facts of Graphology, as distinct from the newer teachings of psychographology. The mastery of the information contained in this division is necessary before you can get the most out of analyzing character from handwriting. Once you have this material absorbed you will be able to advance down the road of any of the fields of modern applied psychology.

Summary

Obviously, the suggestions made in this chapter illustrating ways to analyze yourself and others through your handwriting are only scratches on the surface. The more you find out about the variations in personality patterns the more you will want to know. There is actually no limit to the scope and depth of self-analysis through handwriting study and its practical application in living and working with other people. As long as you remain interested in other people you will find satisfaction in being able to look at specimens of their handwriting and finding out what their personalities are like. You can continuously use this hidden knowledge about others to make your life happier through an understanding of your fellow humans.

Use the "Grapho-Guides" to get a general picture of people and the personality type section to classify people. The Graphology section, complete with the basic principles of handwriting analysis, can be skimmed over in your first reading and referred to later as the occasion demands.

Grapho-Guides

Run a sample of your handwriting through these Grapho-Guides for a quick picture of your personality.

MATURITY SCALE

Explanation

The root of some of your unhappiness may be in the fact that you are not mature enough to adjust easily to unpleasant situations. You are still holding on to childish traits, such as feeling sorry for yourself, "blowing your top," evading issues instead of facing them, and bragging about your accomplishments.

The chart below will not tell you very much in a detailed way but it will indicate just how far advanced you are on the MATURITY SCALE.

CHILDISH WRITING
Rounded small *m's* and *n's*.

sooner. To my was standing

MATURE WRITING
Angular *m's* and *n's*.

Billy Graham

WHAT IT ALL MEANS

Childish

1. If this is the writing of a youngster of 14 or less, it means he is undergoing the normal process of *growing up* and is proceeding normally.
2. If an adult's writing, he is emotionally unstable, has neurotic tendencies, and is apt to be lazy.
3. Must be taught to be a good citizen.
4. Drives his car with little regard for other people.

Mature

1. Master of his environment.
2. Makes his own decisions.
3. Has ability to understand other person's viewpoint.
4. Enjoys being a good citizen.
5. Understands and practices courteous and considerate driving.

FRUSTRATION FINDER

Explanation

You can find out in a few minutes whether or not that frustrated feeling you may have is due to actual psychological frustration or if it is just plain disappointment which will be gone in a short time.

Frustration works one of two ways with a person, depending upon his personality makeup. If he is an extrovert, that is, if he enjoys people more than things or ideas, then he will be overly-expressive in his handwriting. If he is an introvert, one who prefers his own company to that of others, he will be *more intense* in penning his script.

Any disturbance in rhythm also indicates frustration.

FRUSTRATED

Exaggerated Capitals and Loops.

I would appreciate having possible moment, since I

Extremely small and heavy-pressured writing.

NOT FRUSTRATED

Kindergarten as clothing and other

Capitals not more than than three times as tall as small letters.

Will you kindly cotolog of your

Small writing with normal pressure.

WHAT IT ALL MEANS

Frustrated

1. When you are frustrated you are not able to use your normal nervous energy along lines that you personally want to. You have a feeling of being blocked at every turn. In most cases it has a definite connection with affection of one kind or another.
2. You can overcome frustration by simply setting out and doing the things that will make you happy.

Not Frustrated

1. You have a normal and happy sex life, or the prospect of one.
2. In your mind you have decided on a number of ways that your problems can be solved, and it is up to you to make the choice.

Are You a Positive or Negative Person?

Explanation

Positive people are welcome everywhere because they are out-going in their living. They may be good or bad, but at least they are meeting life head-on and are fitting themselves, their own way, into the human family.

Negative people repel us because they withdraw from life, show coldness toward other people, and generally give the impression that it is not necessary to be expressive toward us.

Obviously, it is best to be positive. Which are you?

Positive People Write Large.

Lola M. Tarbell

Negative People Write Small.

I am sorry your Thin

Is Your Personality in Focus?

Explanation

There is no particular asset to having a set personality, but many people feel better if they can be certain that they have achieved a fair measure of definiteness in their character development.

If your writing is clear and legible your personality is in focus; that is, you are an adult image of your childhood pattern.

Your personality is out of focus if your writing is illegible. This means that your personality pattern is still in the process of forming, and it may be beneficial or otherwise.

Your age has nothing to do with the nature of your personality development. You can be a child at 40. You can be an adult at 14.

Legible Writing—Personality In Focus.

Thank you very

Illegible Writing—Personality Out Of Focus.

I am making seeing my letter

Partly Illegible Writing—Personality Adjusting Its Focus.

My girlfriend and O

What Is Your Margin of Safety?

Explanation

We live in a dangerous world today because of the emphasis on *speed* and the growing *complexity* of our civilization. We must proceed cautiously and we must not get confused, whether while driving a car or in trying to solve a personal problem.

Easy Exhaustion is dangerous because it tempts you to take long chances to get relief and rest. It may cause your death on the highway or while at work. If you tire easily you will write with a light pressure, your letters will vary considerably in size, and your t-crossings will be short and weak.

I am interested in.

High Tension will reduce your margin of safety since you will be concentrating so strongly on your own acts you will forget the rest of the world is moving all about you and there may be a fatal collision. Anything you do will be done with reduced control. You will drive faster, drink more, eat more, and over-express yourself. Physiologically you are out of control.

Fast writing, heavy-pressured letter forms, exaggerated capitals, and i-dots made like commas indicate a person who is over-tense.

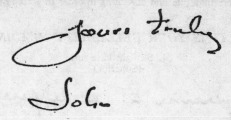

Emotion Matcher

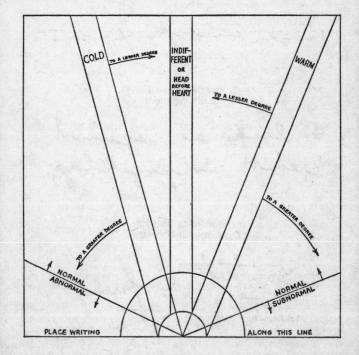

How to Use the Emotion Matcher

1. Place sample of writing along the line at the bottom of the chart.
2. Determine the slant of the writing, indicating the degree of emotional expression, by observing with which section of the chart the upper loop letters (l, h, d) are parallel.
3. Try more than one line of writing in order to get an average.

WHAT IS YOUR RELIABILITY READING?

1. Straight base line.
   (Superior)

reference to a different

2. Wavy base line.
   (Poor)

would need for 4 points

3. Irregular base line.
   (Easily tempted)

*I lack a required
credit in psychology*

4. Wandering base line.
   (Emotions out of control)

*You tell a friend
with him at a*

Explanation

1. Very reliable. Can be trusted to handle money.
2. Unreliable. Careless in handling money but not dishonest.
3. Easily tempted to stray from standard pattern of conduct. Perhaps dishonest. Never should be trusted with money.
4. Mentally ill and therefore cannot be trusted to follow a controlled standard of conduct. Unreliable but not dishonest.

How Is Your Self-respect?

It is important that you maintain your self-respect if you wish to be happy. You must think well of yourself or you cannot expect others to think well of you. People will invariably judge your worth by the value you set on yourself.

You must think well of yourself, but not so well that it is an inflated estimate. Likewise you should never feel inferior. You are as human as anyone else. What better common denominator could you have?

1. If your CAPITAL I is smaller in size than the rest of your capitals, then you do not believe in yourself sufficiently.

2. If your CAPITAL I is the same size or slightly larger than your other capitals, then you have a reasonable self-respect.

3. If your CAPITAL I is much larger than the other capitals, your self-esteem is exaggerated and you will be conceited. If you are an out-going person as well, you will tend to annoy other people, hence this is a trait to tone down if you have it.

Are You Original, Ordinary, or Odd?

The general style of your handwriting will tell you if you are original and creative or if you merely imitate or copy other people or their ideas. It will also point you out as peculiar or eccentric.

Most people in the world are average in the amount of originality they possess. The truly original amount to only a small percentage of the population. The creative persons generally take the leadership, at least in the local situations in which they are concerned. The ordinary citizen steps into line and follows.

Eccentric individuals are even fewer than the original persons. We call them "odd," "queer," "unusual," or "different." Sometimes their eccentricity is masked as originality and their leadership is inflicted upon whole nations who are asked to rally to their "new" ideas.

1. *Ordinary* . . . Writing formed the same as taught in school.

I'm sorry I was

2. *Original* . . . Original letter forms, especially capitals.

Dear Mr Holder

3. *Odd* . . . Exaggeration of letter forms, with a tendency to be ornate.

in Photography
And J Howie
Rare A.

Note: An "odd" person may be a genius, mentally ill or a mental defective, a criminal, or merely a person who has limited his creativity to one phase of life, thus calling public attention to his originality by its very extravagance.

How Is Your Drive?

Success in life is strongly dependent upon the amount of useful energy you can muster up to meet each day's demands. It is more than a matter of simple good health. It is more a possession of what psychologists call "drive."

You may have ambition, but you must also have the power-house of dogged determination to energize your mind into action. Strong energy in motion is *drive*.

A quick study of the pressure of your writing will tell you how much drive you can claim.

1. *Light pressure.* Completely lacking in drive.

Very truly yours,

2. *Medium pressure.* Average drive. Mildly successful.

*This Summer.
Something Or
Theatre because*

3. *Heavy pressure.* Strong drive. Highly successful in anything tried.

*Dear Sir:
In the Spring
published by the United*

Special note

(a) Add *hooks* to heavy pressure and your drive turns to irritating aggressiveness which will interfere with your full success.

(b) Add *over-size capital letters* and your drive becomes selective and you become selfish and self-centered. You will be successful but you will be very unhappy because of the many people you will have "stepped upon" in your climb to the top.

3. How to analyze yourself through your handwriting

What kind of personality do you have?

Now you can study your handwriting and discover the kind of personality that you have. Since there are literally hundreds of ways of classifying people, that is exactly the approach that has been taken in this book. Using the information compiled in these pages you will be able to look at yourself in so many different ways and in so many varying lights that you will certainly end up with an accurate and inclusive portrait of yourself. The measuring stick will be a sample of your handwriting. The analysis will cost you nothing, but it may mean a fortune to you if you use this valuable new knoweldge wisely.

Are you over-aggressive toward others?

We live in a civilization marked by aggression. Some people have allowed the spirit of our age to make them over-aggressive. If you are too aggressive, you will be distasteful to many persons you meet and this will interfere with your achievement, success, and other advancement. Check your writing for aggressive tendencies, such as an extreme forward slant, angular letter forms, heavy pressure, heavily-shaded style of writing, lance-like t-crossings, and your ending strokes carried almost straight down instead of finishing straight out or curled upward.

Free yourself from frustration

Why be frustrated? You are frustrated if you would like to do something that would please you but you avoid doing it because some other person, some situation connected with your home habits or your work routine, or possibly some vaguely understood restrictive fear prevents you from completing in an active way what in your mind you are certain is a pleasant bit of behavior. You should not be frustrated if there is a way to escape from this mental jail. Frustration is an attitude of mind and as such can be changed. If you know you can get rid of frustrated feelings you have made a beginning in freeing yourself.

The sad reality about frustrated people is that one tiny frustration encourages other frustrations until these persons are sour, unhappy bundles of unsatisfied longings.

The only way to get rid of frustrated feelings is to start doing what you *think* you cannot do. If it turns out that you really are not able to do it successfully you will no longer worry about it. If you get real satisfaction from your activity you will have found new personal freedom.

The signs of a frustrated personality

Observe your writing for the following signs of a frustrated personality. One sign means at least some frustration is present in your life; if all signs are seen in your writing you should start this very minute to fight your way through to freedom.

1. Cramped, small writing.
2. t-bars short, even-pressured, and crossed low on the stem.
3. Hooks, catches, and backward movements in writing.
4. Backhand writing combined with heavy-pressured small writing.
5. Narrow, close writing in a large hand.
6. Printed writing in a small hand, combined with heavy pressure.
7. Vertical writing in a medium hand combined with large, flourishing capitals.
8. Capital I made with a single stroke, heavy-pressured.
9. Small letters tied with tight knots.
10. Small a's and o's tightly closed.
11. Signature encircled with a large loop.

Your fears may be without foundation

When fear becomes a major factor in coloring an individual's personality it needs to be studied so that it can be unseated from its place of dominance. Your handwriting will reveal just how afraid you are, and this may be a segment of psychological knowledge that you may not have been aware of. You may have attributed your fearful way of living to some other cause, a cause which you may have told yourself you could not help or control.

Before examining your writing, let us take a swift trip into the realm of fear. In its mildest form, fear is doubt. In its most frightful form it is terror. Between these extremes we have feelings of misery, nervousness, confused excitement, insecurity, inadequacy, and like emotions or emotional reactions. Because fear is an emotion, it is induced either by ourselves or by a fear-stimulating environment.

Fears which you create yourself can be stopped by yourself. It may be difficult to remove fears produced by your environment. By removing the environment, or by taking yourself away from the environment, you can even erase these fears.

Most fears, of any sort, are unfounded. There are many fears based on sheer ignorance. Knowledge will remove them. Misconceptions breed scores of fears which clear-minded people are never bothered by. Narrowness of mind, or the inability to put ourselves in the other person's place, causes another group of unfounded fears. Insults to our own built-up ego may bring on a whole series of unjustified anxieties. Sex rivalry even stimulates some persons to be afraid.

Characteristics of fear in handwriting

If your handwriting reveals any of the following characteristics you will be subject to one or more bad effects of unfounded fear.

1. Poor rhythm in writing, suggesting lack of muscular co-ordination.
2. Uncontrolled variation in pen pressure.
3. Extreme variations in size of small letters.
4. Any expression of nervousness in writing, from "loose nerves" resulting in undue lightening of pressure, to "tight nerves" causing sudden intensification of pressure.
5. Inability to hold a pen steady enough to write a complete sentence.

Some special advice on fear for certain kinds of people

1. If you write a vertical hand, indicating reserve and possible timidity, you should practice doing some of the things you have in the past been afraid to do. Get rid of the fear habit.

2. If you write with original letter formations and flourished capitals, you have a tendency to fear the imaginary, which is a sheer waste of time. Your lively and reactive personality will prevent you from removing fear entirely, but you should confine your fears to those which are real.

3. If you write with an uneven base line and if you vary your small letters too much, you mostly fear insecurity. Strive for security and thus get rid of a prime cause of your unhappiness.

4. If you write with a heavy-pressured angular hand, with lance-like t-crossings, you have the bad habit of reacting to fear by wanting to fight. Keep your emotions under control and you will suffer no ill effects.

5. If you have a lot of hooks in your handwriting, you allow each new fear to stir up old fears, thus multiplying your anxieties. Live with your fears one at a time and you will be able to handle them better.

6. If you write a conventional, unoriginal hand with the capitals made so simple they are almost print-like, you are in a continual state of a dread of the unknown. You anticipate fear. You should save your anticipation for pleasant experiences and soon there will be nothing to fear.

Check yourself for these likeable personality qualities

1. Sincerity	Straight lines; small letters of equal size; ungraceful hand; letters in words increase in size occasionally.
2. Spontaneity	Downstrokes shaded; upper strokes long; cross strokes never descending.
3. Friendliness	Letters extended; m and n like w and u.
4. Dependability	Straight lines; letters all same size.
5. Determination	Long, firm t-bars; lower loop letters ending in strokes instead of loops.
6. Adaptability	Uneven base line; angular writing.
7. Conversational Ease	Smooth-running hand; d and t looped.
8. Broadmindedness	Words and lines well-spaced.

People will dislike you if you possess these qualities

1. Insincerity	Decreasing size of letters in words; hasty writing in backhand style.

2. Dishonesty   Small a and o open at the bottom; uneven line of writing.

3. Carelessness   Loop letters of one line running into lines above and below; careless punctuation; t's crossed many ways and carelessly.

4. Coldness (Emotional coolness)   Backhand writing in the angular hand; writing medium or large in size; light-pressured writing tending toward conventional letter forms.

5. Weakness of Will   t's crossed very lightly; i's dotted with comma-like mark instead of dot.

6. Narrow-mindedness   Words close together; crowded spacing; letters never extended.

7. Stinginess   Angular, crowded writing. All letters small; terminal strokes absent.

8. Licentiousness   Muddy, pasty-looking, heavy writing; strokes coarse and irregular.

Watch out for emotional storm warnings

Your handwriting is your own personal barometer for emotional storm warnings. The pressure in your script will change according to rise or fall of your feelings. You have perhaps noticed that when you dash off a note in anger you write faster than usual. A closer examination will reveal to you that you also increase the pen pressure. In addition, t-crossings will be made longer than usual, i-dots will be made like commas, and rightward-leaning writing will take on a greater slant.

When you observe that your pressure is consistently getting heavier, you can be sure that your emotions are beginning to influence your daily activities to a larger degree. It also means that there will be an increase in stress and strain, thus making it easier for you to become mentally or physically ill. Tenseness will take over as logical reasoning is relegated to the background. The remedy for this danger is to take more time out for reflective thinking to give you ample opportunity for taking stock of yourself. You need to slow yourself down to prevent your emotions from racing you ahead.

Emotions add need color to living, but when they are not controlled they only confuse.

Increase in pressure to the point of heaviness also indicates over-emphasis on material things such as the acquisition of money and taking one's work too seriously.

The lighter your pen pressure the healthier you are liable to be. If your pressure varies from day to day between light and heavy you need someone's help to get you back on an even keel.

Summary

In analyzing yourself you must believe what you find out about yourself from your handwriting. You must also decide to do something about correcting any faults you discover. You will find life pleasanter when you know how you look to other people, seeing behind your own personal prejudices. Foolish mental fogs caused by frustrations and fears will disappear and life will be brighter as you get a clear picture of life's interesting relationships.

Happiness was meant for you, regardless of your station or condition. Knowing yourself truly will enrich your own mental outlook. Knowing what the rest of your friends and associates are like will enable you to live with them easily because you will understand them as individuals and you will be able to adjust to them as individuals. You will be accepted everywhere. Who could dislike a person who understood him better than he knew himself?

M. F. Ashley Montagu . . . Handwriting Analysis

Dear Mr Holder:

I am glad you liked "The Natural Superiority of Women." It gave me much pleasure to write it — but I am astonished to find what opposition it has aroused among so many men! Every fact stated in the book is easily confirmed, but there seem to be few men who are willing to check the facts before dismissing them to me overpowering evidence of the facts.

Alas, I will not be at Chautauqua this summer, but I do hope to come again.

With best wishes,

Sincerely yours,

M F Ashley Montagu

The author of the best seller, *The Natural Superiority of Women,* has a preponderance of masculine traits. Dr. Montagu writes with a firm, insistent pressure, indicating his forcefulness, aggressive spirit, and dogged determination—all distinctly male attributes. His well-spaced writing denotes a feeling for design and spatial relationships and a desire to simplify the complex. Originality and creative urge are seen in the "different" formations of certain capital letters, such as the "D" and "W." His innate sense of modesty is revealed by the straight line formation of the capital "I." Because of Dr. Montagu's strong likes and dislikes, and due also to his habit of airing his ideas with such a high degree of dramatic definiteness, he falsely impresses those who do not know him as one who has an exalted self-esteem. Actually, he is unassuming when he is moving about in his regular round of activities and prefers to remain in the background of events. Being a true scientist and scholar, it disturbs his conscience not to speak up, and with vigor, when truth is being disturbed by those less familiar with the facts.

His intuitive sense is indicated by the occasional breaks in his words, while his appreciation for color and music are seen in the heavy-pressured script which is also naturally shaded. He has the type of personality that cannot be concealed; it is electric, inspiring, and impinging. In other words, when he enters a room people turn around to see who has come in. The atmosphere has been changed!

He has a tremendous capacity for details, with the scientist's ability to organize them and draw necessary conclusions: his well-formed small letters, the way two words are at times joined together with a connecting-stroke bridge, and his consistent style of writing, all point in that direction.

Dr. Montagu has one important weakness: He has to contend with the strong feelings of a sentimentalist while trying to maintain complete objectivity in his work. His dramatic script, the protective, sweeping rhythms of individual words —but not of entire lines of writing—denote a person who is influenced by human relations in no small way. Another manner of stating this point would be to say that he is close to Nature at all times since he dislikes pure theory without any practical application.

His dwindling ending strokes on some words and his tendency to write larger as he pens other words suggests that he seesaws between being shrewdly diplomatic on some occasions and excessively frank on others.

His sense of humor is rich and earthy but never out of harmony with the good taste of the situation, which does not rule out a ribald reaction where it would do no harm. This is clear because of his heavy-pressured and rough-edged "i" dots.

He enjoys being dramatic, as evidenced by the heavy spurts of strong pressure throughout his script. He is happiest with a small circle of friends since his philosophy of life looks upon extroversion as a waste of human energy. Dr. Montagu's vertical writing, combined with the unadorned capital letters, for the most part, make it plain that he prefers to save his social gestures for groups which are small enough in size so that the members of the groups will be able to benefit from the human interchange and interplay.

Note: After receiving this analysis, Dr. Montagu made the following comment:

Excellent!

Ashley Montagu

Part 2

The way you write and what it means

4. Graphology: the meanings
in the different ways
that people write

Graphology, or handwriting analysis, as it is more popularly known, is the science of discovering a person's character and personality by examining his handwriting. European countries, notably France and England, accept the testimony of graphologists as legitimate court evidence, thereby giving the science authority. In some of the European universities, Graphology is listed as one of the subjects taught, and in our own country numerous experiments have been carried on in psychological research centers to discover uses for this science in the field of personality guidance.

Raymond Trillat, of the Psycho-Pedagogic Center of the University of Paris, in addition to carrying on his career as a practicing graphologist advising business firms on personnel selection, also has been experimenting with the use of handwriting therapy to treat children for emotional ills.

Enough has been found by American experimenters and psychologists to admit the unmistakable relationship between a person's handwriting and his character.

Nothing is included in the following pages making up the Graphology text which I have not personally found to be true through comparative handwriting studies and personality analysis in my 20 years experience.

Remember that the real worth of the graphological material that follows is in the way you use it, with what you know about modern psychology, to improve yourself and to understand others.

This is the new science of *Psychographology*.

Some Basic Principles of Handwriting Analysis

Principle of neutralization

Every handwriting will show some contradictory signs, but this should not be allowed to confuse you. Apply the principle of neutralization; that is, one graphological sign may neutralize or cancel out the effect of another graphological sign if both signs are present in equal numbers. If one sign indicates selfishness and another denotes unselfishness it means that the person possesses both characteristics in average proportions so that actually they neutralize each other. If a person's script shows that he is both selfish and unsefish then, in reality, he is neither. Strongly selfish and heroically unselfish individuals will not write average hands but will write according to their character.

Principle of support

When a person is strongly endowed with a particular character trait there will be two or more signs in the handwriting indicating this fact. This is known as the principle of support. The more signs that are present tending to support the existence of a trait of character, the stronger is that particular trait. Strong traits are usually habitual with a person whereas weak traits are displayed only occasionally.

If the weak trait is a flattering one then it is displayed only when the person possessing it is in a very good humor, most always when everything is going his way. If the weak trait is a derogatory one then it is displayed only when the person having it loses control of his feelings, that is, when he is angry or unduly excited.

Some Secrets of Slant

Forward movement

When a person writes with his handwriting slanting to the right he is executing a natural movement or gesture. He is allowing himself full expression, working freely with no restrictions. That is why a person who writes like that is natural and sympathetic. He leans out toward others and is quite apt to be emotional since he allows his feelings to direct him.

Handwriting sloping to the right would also indicate that the person writing in that manner would be the kind who would like to express himself. He would allow his emotions to dictate his actions. The more his handwriting slanted to the right the more he would be liable to let himself go. People who freely express themselves are often very demonstrative in their affections since this is their way of satisfying the basic need of love.

Movement and emotion

The continuous action which natural and free expression necessitates tends to discourage an emotionally excited person from calming his emotions once they have been aroused. This is true because it is difficult to stop when one is moving forward at a steady, swift, and rhythmic pace. Regardless of what he is doing, if a person is filled with ardor and enthusiasm, he will find it hard to stop when he is being carried along on the swift current of his emotions.

A natural person responds readily

A natural person is more open to suggestion than one who is unnatural because a natural person does not set up any artificial barriers or objections that might neutralize or turn aside another's suggestions.

Forward-writing people are easily made to do things since their naturalness places them in a mood favorable for starting at the slightest suggestion. Natural people take others at their word, falling prey to propaganda pleas, believing all advertising, and judging the world by the way it appears to them.

Unrestrained feelings will over-rule reason

People who allow themselves complete and full expression of their emotions are apt to be swayed to decisions by their feelings and not by their reasoning powers.

The most natural way of life is to be guided by your feelings since this is most in accordance with the Nature that is all about us. The civilized reasoning ability that we are all so proud of was developed by experience and has led more and more to unnaturalness and artificiality as we have progressed in reasoning things out. As we think we tend to act, with Man always delighting to disagree with Nature and acting in his own chosen way. Man was guided by his reason when he constructed factories; were he directed by his feelings he might have been content to remain in the agricultural state.

People who are very expressive emotionally write with a very decided rightward slant, picturing in their handwriting the excess of freedom that they crave and yield to.

Self-control in writing

If to write with a forward slant to one's writing is the most natural and also the easiest way to write, then writing that is vertical must be the result of a conscious control on the part of the writer. He deliberately keeps himself from writing naturally. This act of his is prompted by an inner desire to hold back his natural expression and this feeling is carried over into his handwriting.

The very fact that he is thinking about what he is doing shows that he acts not on impulse but rather as the result of deliberation. His emotions do not rule his judgments. If they did his writing would be written with a natural, forward slope. He weighs the arguments for each action, pro and con, rather than succumbing to sentiment.

Wiser action results from reasoning

A person who consciously controls himself from allowing his feelings to have full sway over his actions will tend to make many more right judgments than one who is ruled by impulse.

People who are always "flying off the handle" and who are easily excited are apt to do things according to the dictates of their feelings, not considering their actions in the light of reason. Their judgments naturally will be warped to some degree because they will have nothing to set right their off-balance, bringing them back to an even keel. If they examined both sides of a question, as they would if they stopped to think things through, they would be able to arrive at a fair conclusion.

Actions resulting from previous thoughtful consideration are wiser than those arising from a mere impulse since the one is the balance between two divergent opinions, whereas the other can only be the way one would act if he allowed his feelings to guide him. Only one viewpoint is considered. There is no way for this viewpoint to be balanced or to be modified and if one's emotions happen to direct one's thoughts along wrong lines then the judgment will be poor.

Backhand writing

People who write backhand exercise a great deal of self-restraint because it takes even more effort and more conscious control to write this way than to write vertically. People who write backhand usually think of themselves first and are not naturally generous.

Individuals who control their emotions so well that they only do things which their reason dictates that they may, will tend to be selfish. Backhand writers are of this sort. They know the reason for everything they do and never do anything they do not want to do. This increases their selfishness since, if they only do things to benefit themselves, they will not be evaluating things from the other person's viewpoint. There are very few situations that help others just because they help us.

Writers of the backhand style also are critical because they study life's happenings with an impersonal approach. They lose the beneficial effect gained from taking a sympathetic, emotionally-colored attitude to at least some of the day's events. Devoid of naturalness they find it difficult to meet others halfway but wait cautiously for them to make all the advances.

Warning!

Handwriting reveals the true character and personality of an individual but it cannot tell you the exact details of what that individual has experienced in his lifetime. It will indicate how that person has been affected by environment and by his heredity but it will not divulge the specific nature of any past happenings or conditions.

For instance, the writing of an individual may show that he is unusually shy, but it will give no real clue as to the *real* cause of the shyness. By building up a composite personality picture of an individual from examining various signs seen in script you may be able to guess at the kind of situation which could have caused the shyness, but you would never be absolutely sure. For that reason, the beginner in handwriting analysis should concern himself with the use of Psychographology as a useful aid to self-discovery rather than as an infallible pen portrait of the past.

Everyone's life is different just as everyone's writing differs. Five hundred greedy persons have five hundred different sets of circumstances and backgrounds accounting for their individual patterns of greediness. The psychographologist must be content with finding out the simple fact that they are greedy and then use that information in a constructive or profitable way.

When *you* find out all about yourself and others by looking at handwriting you will be more interested in the future of things than in historical background. Handwriting analysis cannot reveal the direction of future events except to point out the common-sense conclusions apt to occur if events follow normal courses. If handwriting reveals that a person is dishonest it would be fair to assume that sooner or later that person will yield to temptation and be in trouble, more or less serious, depending upon how the situation fits in with other situations impinging upon it. A forger may pass a hundred checks and get away with each forgery, until he writes out one more check, after which he is caught—simply because no one detected his forgeries in the first 100 bogus check signings.

Explanation for the pages that follow

The material in the following pages has been set down in tabular form, with illustrations situated close to the graphological explanations for convenient and quick reference. There is no need to memorize or master all of these facts. The usefulness of this organization of handwriting analysis signs is in helping you to delve into the details of Graphology. With this information as a sound base you can progress to psychographology by adding what you have learned about psychology.

Slope

1. *Forward slanting writing. Writing slants to the right about 45 degrees.* Denotes a friendly, affectionate nature.

To know the cast
have sent this.

2. *Forward slanting to a marked degree. Writing slants to the right as much as it possibly can without becoming horizontal.* Denotes a person very affectionate in nature and one who places the heart before the head in most important decisions.

Communication !(2)

(3) Investments con

3. Vertical writing. Writing does not slant either to the left or to the right but assumes a vertical position.

Denotes a person who has a good measure of self-control and who is the master of his emotions. His head rules his heart.

I am hoping to spend the

4. Backhand writing. Writing slants to the left.

Denotes a person secretive, introspective, and one not apt to be very sincere in his demonstrations of affection.

sessions? I am interested

Form

1. Copybook. Almost exact copy of style of handwriting taught in school.

Denotes an imitative, unoriginal nature. Commonplace personality. One with no ideas of his own.

I have a friend

2. Conventional. Unoriginal letter formations with no attempt at any individuality.

Denotes a conventional nature. Not apt to do anything particularly outstanding. Afraid to do things on his own initiative.

for the next four

3. Flourished. Flourished capital letters and long ending strokes on small letters. Writing large and pretentious.

Denotes an extravagant and adventurous nature. One paying little attention to details. Great imagination and self-esteem.

Please send

Summer Courses

4. Awkward. Writing sprawls over page and is ill-formed. Motor control of writing movement is lacking.

Denotes a slow-moving, illogical mind. One apt to be careless in his thinking.

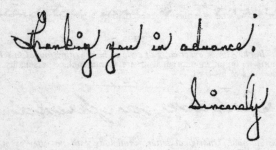

I am interested and another subject

5. Ornate. Writing is dressed up with unnecessary curleycues.

Denotes a fussy nature paying too much attention to unnecessary details.

Thanking you in advance!

Sincerely

Loops

1. Loops long above line and short below.

Denotes an idealistic nature.

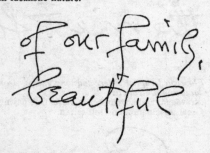

of our family, beautiful

2. Loops short above line and long below.

Denotes a businesslike, material nature.

information regarding

3. *Loop letters well developed both above and below line.*
Denotes a strong imagination. An enterprising nature.

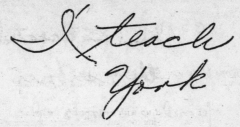

4. *Lower loops reaching into line below.*
Denotes one who is restless and speculative. Romantically inclined. One fond of new ideas.

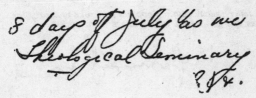

5. *Upstroke of lower loop letters curve well to left.*
Denotes a clannish nature.

6. *Lower loops wide and inflated.*
Denotes one gifted with imagination and cleverness.

7. *Lower loops long and rounded.*
Denotes the culture-minded person.

8. Lower loops made with stroke.
Denotes a conservative nature. One who is practical, systematic, firm, and self-reliant.

early vegly

9. Lower loops made with firm, heavy strokes.
Denotes a strong, determined nature; one hard to convince.

family consists of

Loop Letters

1. Small letter f made with no loop, return stroke to the right.
Denotes one desirous of getting things done quickly.

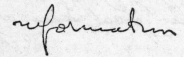

2. Small letter f made with round, inflated loops.
Denotes one fond of pleasure; a buoyant and carefree nature. One lacking in deep thought.

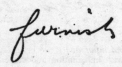

3. Small letter f made with return stroke turned sharply to the left.
Denotes a vindictive, revengeful disposition. One inclined to be lazy.

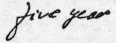

4. Small letter g made with stroke instead of loop.
Denotes a determined mind.

leading

5. *Small g made with return stroke to the right.*
Denotes a generous, kind nature.

6. *Loop of small g made unduly long.*
Denotes a person with a strong tendency to exaggerate.

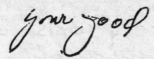

7. *Small letters g and y made with flourishes within loop.*
Denotes a tendency toward moral weakness.

8. *Small letters g and y end with stroke and tiny hook.*
Denotes a persevering nature.

Pressure

1. *Heavy pressured writing, firmly made strokes with or without shading.*
Denotes one with assurance and aggressiveness. One lacking in delicacy and possessing an exacting and domineering disposition. One who is selfish, vain, and inconsiderate unless refined by much education.

2. *Heavy pressured writing, thick and large.*
Denotes one who is deceitful and revengeful; rough and bold in deportment. Marked talents along certain lines. Self-reliant.

3. Heavy pressured writing, large, muddy and sloppy.

Denotes a sensual nature; one with strong passions and an animal appetite.

4. Light pressured writing, total absence of shading; all downstrokes made lightly, and without pressure.

Denotes a temperate nature; one with a quiet and simple disposition. High sense of honor. Kindly nature. One with little craving for physical pleasures.

5. Unconsciously shaded writing.

Denotes an insistent nature. One with natural executive ability. One who desires all the good things of life and who is willing to work for them.

6. Consciously shaded writing, downstrokes made deliberate and heavy to make the writing beautiful.

Denotes an affected, egotistical nature. One lacking in good taste, weak in character and possessing a poor intellect.

Capitals

1. Capitals large and out of proportion to small letters. (More than three times as high.)

Denotes an egotistical, conceited person. One loving display. Possessing a strong sense of pride.

2. *Capitals small—not more than twice the size of the small letters.*
Denotes a timid nature; one lacking in self-esteem.

Albert H B

3. *Capitals unusually ornamented.*
Denotes one ostentatious in manner and of mediocre talents. Shallow intellect.

4. *Capitals plain and almost printlike.*
Denotes a modest, refined nature, with cultural tastes.

Dear Sirs,
I am.

5. *Capitals made plain and large.*
Denotes a self-reliant nature. Strong sense of personal pride.

A Closed

6. *Incurve present in capitals.* (*The incurve is an initial stroke preceding the making of the letter, passing from right to left.*)
Denotes one with a high opinion of himself coupled with a strong sensitiveness in regard to social position.

Mrs

7. *Capitals made with heavy pressure.*
Denotes one loving pleasure and comfort.

Mrs.
I am interested.

8. Capitals made very plain.
Denotes a keen mind.

9. Capitals made plain, angular, and awkward looking.
Denotes a plain, unemotional, tactless nature.

10. Capitals printed.
Denotes a person with constructive ability; one with an exacting nature.

Capital Letter M

1. First stroke of M higher than others.
Denotes one proud of family name and social position; independent.

2. Second or third stroke of M highest.
Denotes a nervous, erratic, unreasonable person; hard to get along with. Extra-imaginative.

3. M made with three vertical strokes and one horizontal stroke.
Denotes one who likes nice things; refined tastes.

4. M elaborately looped on incurve or at end of third stroke.
Denotes an ostentatious, uncultured nature.

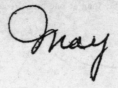

5. Incurve on M swings from right to left cutting through letter.
Denotes a sensitive, self-appreciative nature. One who is proud and
self-reliant.

Size

1. Very small writing, so small that it is very hard to read.
Denotes an extremely introspective person; one not apt to be very
communicative or to have any really close friends.

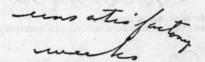

*2. Small writing, smaller than one is accustomed to seeing on letters one
receives, but not unusually small.*
Denotes a scientific mind.

*3. Medium sized writing, writing which is the size one sees on most letters
one receives.*
Denotes a person with average tastes, ideas, and desires. One easy to
get along with and one not apt to expect too much of a person. Practical
and materialistic; leaning toward the physical type.

4. *Large writing, definitely too large for the sheet on which it appears.*
   Denotes an extroverted person, one who is not happy unless he is surrounded by plenty of friends. One who finds it difficult to concentrate. Restless nature, can't stay long at one task. Veneer personality, close to surface.

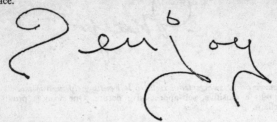

5. *Large, flourished writing with deliberate shading.*
   Denotes a boasting, pompous nature.

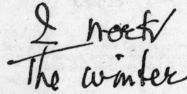

6. *Abnormally large and angular writing.*
   Denotes one easily excited and possessed with tremendous enthusiasm. Self-willed.

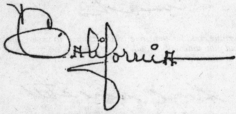

7. *Variable in size. Small letters of varying sizes ranging from one-sixteenth inch upwards.*
   Denotes a childish, immature nature. One who is the complete servant of his feelings. One apt to be credulous, self-centered, and over-expressive. Thoughtless of other people's feelings. Indecisive.

Margins

1. Margins wide on both sides.

Denotes an artistic, aesthetic nature. One who likes harmony and order. Original in ideas. One who would be very fussy over details.

I have read of the Writers & Workshop in Saturday Review, and

2. Left margin beginning wide and ending narrow.

Denotes one who likes to spend money but successfully checks this tendency.

Gentlemen
Wo
about the C
the Weekly,
Plea
houses uva
month, dun
family comp

3. Left margin beginning narrow and ending wide.
Denotes one who likes to save but who cannot hold on to his money.

4. Uneven left margin.
Denotes a lively, careless nature. One lacking in system.

5. No margins used; all space available for writing made use of.
Denotes a stingy, parsimonious nature. Lacking in good taste and untidy in appearance.

Legibility

1. Legible writing.
Denotes a slow but accurate thinker.

to be the best would go all

2. Illegible writing.
Denotes a fast, less accurate thinker. Strong individuality.
NOTE: Illegibility is the result of rapid writing wherein the pen tries to keep pace with a speedy flow of thoughts.

knowledge of piano wealth of experience

Punctuation

1. Absence of punctuation. Punctuation is lacking occasionally. Small t's left uncrossed here and there, with an occasional i or j undotted.
Denotes an absent-minded nature. One apt to be late in keeping appointments. One lacking in caution and negligent of details.

Registrar Chautauqua Chautauqua New York

*2. Careful punctuation. Small t's crossed with precise stroke and small
i's and j's dotted with even-pressured, heavy dots.*

Denotes a person who will hold you to the letter of your agreements
with him. One who can be depended upon to function well in an emergency. A very orderly nature.

> I improve . We have stopped all
> his extra curricular activities
> for this next marking period—

*3. Careless punctuation. Small t's left uncrossed more than half the time;
also, small i's left undotted, and commas left out.*

Denotes a thoughtless nature. Apt to be lacking in tact and liable to
make many costly mistakes. Not to be depended upon in an emergency.

*4. Dashes used in place of periods. Dashes of varying lengths used in
place of periods to fill out line of words.*

Denotes a practical nature; one not easily fooled. Aggressive.

> mind workshop
> in conducting —

5. Periods made quickly resembling elongated dashes.

Denotes an excitable nature. Never found in a refined hand.

> except my walking.

6. Periods made round and deliberate.

Denotes a calm disposition.

> n pg.
> do all the religions.
> Christianity)—

7. *Frequent use of exclamation, interrogation, quotation marks, and underscore.*

Denotes one who is romantically inclined. One who becomes easily enthused over things claiming his personal interest.

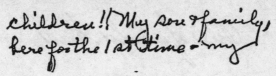

children!! My son & family, here for the 1st time — my

8. *Needless and constant use of quotation marks.*
Denotes an odd nature; one weak in intellect.

9. *Accurate use of punctuation, especially colon and semicolon.*
Denotes one with literary ability or training.

She is interested in

music e.g. piano.

10. *Comma habitually left out.*
Denotes a confused mind.

11. *Words often underlined.*
Denotes a feeling for accuracy, but also, a tendency to exaggerate.

Sports

Dancing

12. *Words or phrases set off in parentheses.*
Denotes a capricious nature; one possessing delicate feelings.

"King & I" (movie)

listen or oblige

Uniformity

1. Small letters all same size.
Denotes a consistent person.

Our family has

2. Small letters of varying sizes.
Denotes a person having a taste for change and variety. One not to be depended upon in an emergency.

Please send me

3. Small letters decreasing in size at end of word.
Denotes a tactful, diplomatic person. One who does not tell you everything that is on his mind.

may have concerning

4. Small letters larger at end of word.
Denotes a conscientious nature. One with high personal standards. Honest and straightforward. One easily imposed upon.

5. Small letters slurred and only half-formed.
Denotes one who is impatient with unimportant details; hates fuss and bother. One who likes to get things finished as quickly as possible. An evasive and secretive nature.

thanking you for your

Strokes

1. Cross strokes light; no shading.
Denotes a nature devoid of sensuousness.

Gentlemen:

2. Cross strokes heavy and shaded.
Denotes one sensuous to music, art, and human emotions.

the reavards and artistically

3. Initial stroke absent in letter.
Denotes one patient and self-controlled.

for this coming very much.

4. Initial stroke tiny.
Denotes one possessing a quick temper.

interested and like to register.

5. Initial stroke a hook.
Denotes one having a possessive, egotistical nature.

season. So I and practise

6. Initial stroke curved.
Denotes a person with a sense of humor.

happy to send

7. Initial stroke long and inflexible.
Denotes a quarrelsome, impatient person.

so that we may

Connecting Strokes

1. Consistent connections. Connecting strokes always present so that all letters in a word are connected. This includes capitals connected to succeeding small letters.
Denotes a logical, well-ordered mind.

University

2. Connections occasionally broken. Connecting strokes broken in occasional words.
Denotes a flexible mind, willing to welcome new ideas for the very sake of their newness. Combines intuition with reason in making decisions.

music courses,

If possible,

3. Connections entirely disconnected. Connecting strokes broken in each word.
Denotes an intuitive nature; one given to acting according to "hunches" rather than following the dictates of reason.

I am a remedial teacher and would

4. *Words connected.*
Denotes a person with executive ability. A keen and exacting nature.

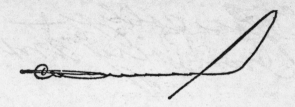

5. *t-crossings connected.*
Denotes a person with a great capacity for getting things done.

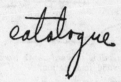

6. *Words connected with continuous sweep of connecting terminal strokes.*
Denotes a stubborn, obstinate nature.

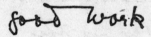

Ending Strokes

1. *Terminal strokes clipped short.*
Denotes a selfish, businesslike approach to life; one who is very prudent and careful.

2. *Terminal strokes made very long.*
Denotes a generous, sympathetic nature.

3. Terminal strokes used to fill otherwise blank spaces.
Denotes a suspicious nature.

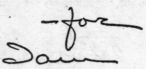

4. Terminal strokes extending long and horizontally.
Denotes a liberal, generous nature seeking to help others.

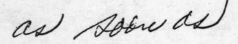

5. Terminal strokes extending upward above word.
Denotes one with a vivid imagination.

6. Terminal strokes turned upward.
Denotes one benevolent and good-natured. One gracious and courteous in manner.

7. Terminal strokes descending without hook.
Denotes a secretive nature.

8. Terminal strokes descending with hook.
Denotes a person opinionated and insistent. One who cannot take orders.

9. Terminal strokes curving backward over word almost enclosing it.
Denotes one with a protective nature; one desirous of shielding others from harm.

Dots (Over i and j)

1. i or j left undotted.

Denotes a lack of memory; one liable to forget important details. A person lacking in concentration. Careless nature.

Oberlin

2. Dot placed close to stem.

Denotes one with a good memory; attentive to details. Lacking in imagination; cautious and careful.

in obtaining

3. Dot placed high and to the right.

Denotes an enthusiastic, vibrant nature; an impulsive disposition.

interested

4. Dot placed to right, not high and not low.

Denotes a happy-go-lucky person; impatient and thoughtless.

this is

5. Dot placed to left, but not above stem.

Denotes a deliberate nature; a slow thinker. Apt to be over-careful and too cautious.

Will

6. Dot made light and firm.

Denotes one with moral courage; a person who dares to do what he thinks is right.

7. Large and heavy dot.

Denotes one who likes the world and its pleasures.

8. Circle dot.
Denotes a natural faddist; one who has a taste for design.

Miss Louise

9. Dot comma-like and irregular.
Denotes an irritable disposition.

stiffness.

10. Dot made like horizontal dash.
Denotes an energetic nature.

first

11. Dot made like descending dash.
Denotes a courageous nature; one with strong opinions.

Sincerely

12. Dot made like wavy dash.
Denotes a light-hearted, fun-loving nature.

in

13. Dot made club-shaped.
Denotes a brutal, mean, sensual nature.

Jessie

Small Letters (a and o)

1. a and o open at the top.
Denotes a talkative nature.

you please
housing

2. a and o closed at the top.
Denotes a person who can keep a secret.

old daughter attend

3. Some a's and o's open at top, some closed.
Denotes a changeable person not to be fully relied upon.

vacation a good

4. a and o knotted at the top.
Denotes a close-mouthed person.

Harold

5. a and o open at the base.
Denotes a dishonest person.

Leo   Ray

Small Letters (m and n)

1. Small m and n made angular, appearing like w and u.
Denotes an adaptable nature; one who is a good mixer; one with a keen perception.

in attending

2. Small m and n made rounded, not appearing like w or u.
Denotes an unadaptable nature; one possessing simple tastes.

and became

Small Letters (p)

1. Lower loop of small p long with full swing to left.
Denotes a lover of the outdoors; physical ableness; one who enjoys exercise.

stamped envelope

2. Stroke or loop of p made long above and short below.
Denotes one lacking in physical strength.

appreciate

3. Lower point of p sharp with upstroke ascending on right of stem.
Denotes an aggressive nature.

please

4. Stroke or loop of p made short above and long below.
Denotes one having muscular strength.

places

5. Lower point of p rounded and ascending upward on left of letter.
Denotes a peace-loving nature.

approximate

T Bars

1. t-crossing made heavy.
Denotes a strong will.

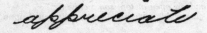

interviews

2. *t-crossing light and careless.*
Denotes a weak will.

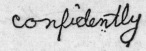

3. *t-crossing made wavy.*
Denotes a flirtatious nature.

4. *t-crossing hooked downward on one end.*
Denotes a determined nature.

5. *t-crossing hooked upward on one end.*
Denotes a vindictive nature.

6. *t-crossing hooked on both ends.*
Denotes a person with an indomitable will that will seldom admit defeat.

7. *t-crossing made very long.*
Denotes an ambitious nature.

8. *t-crossing made very short.*
Denotes a repressed nature.

9. *t-crossing flourished.*
   Denotes a slight eccentricity.

Methodist Home

10. *t-crossing made to left of stem.*
    Denotes a procrastinating nature; an indecisive and weak personality.

informative

11. *t-crossing made to right of stem.*
    Denotes a person full of enthusiasm; impulsive.

like to

12. *t-crossing slanting downward to right.*
    Denotes a pugnacious, argumentative person; expresses his opinion whether wanted or not.

stay on the

13. *t-crossing thick, club-like and slanting downward.*
    Denotes a brutal coarse nature.

t

14. *t-crossing lance-like.*
    Denotes a sarcastic, sharp nature.

truly

15. *t-crossing made with convex curve.*
    Denotes a self-controlled person.

truly

16. t-crossing soaring upward.
  Denotes an ambitious, imaginative nature.

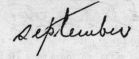

17. t-crossing made with concave curve.
  Denotes a person easily led to an indulgence in physical appetites.

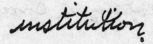

18. t-crossing looped close to stem.
  Denotes a persistent nature.

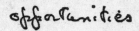

19. t-crossing star-shaped.
  Denotes a super-sensitive nature.

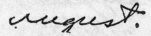

20. t-crossing made above letter.
  Denotes an adventurous, imaginative spirit.

21. t-crossing lacking.
  Denotes a lack of self-confidence.

22. t-crossing gracefully looped.
  Denotes a person with keen sensitivities.

23. *t-crossing made without lifting pen from paper.*
Denotes a sensitive nature.

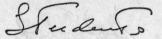

24. *Variety of styles of t-crossings.*
Denotes a person still in the adjustment stage. He is still trying to find which things should be of most importance to him. His philosophy of life is still in a state of flux.

the Catalogue correctly?

That in the case of flute

25. *t carefully crossed.*
Denotes a calm, sure, certain nature.

suggested
sibility

26. *t-stem looped.*
Denotes a talkative disposition. One who takes offense easily.

Western

27. *t-stem pointed instead of looped.*
Denotes a reserved and dignified nature.

story

28. *t-stem open at bottom; tent-shaped.*
Denotes a person deceptive and evasive.

what

29. t-crossings of uniform thickness.
    Denotes a serious, temperate nature.

Talented.
the

Style

1. Angular. Writing has a jagged, angular appearance.
    Denotes a vibrant, energetic personality. One who gets things done. One not happy unless he is busy doing something.

wonderful 3 mth.

and am anxious

2. Rounded. Writing has a soft, rounded appearance. Small letters have curved tops.
    Denotes a sympathetic nature. One easily imposed upon. One apt to be too credulous for his own good.

and where

would

3. Mixed. Combination of angular and rounded writing.
    Denotes a changing personality. Continual conflict between head and heart, selfishness and unselfishness, and between the physical and mental. Unsettled state of mind.

I are sophomores

and would like

Spacing

1. Regular spacing. Spacing between lines and between words, even and consistent.

Denotes a logical, well-balanced mind; suggests good judgment.

2. Irregular spacing. Spacing between lines irregular and inconsistent.

Denotes an illogical mind; suggests poor judgment.

3. Tangled writing. Spacing very irregular with loops of one line running into loops of other lines.

Denotes a confused mind. One lacking in poise, unreliable, and a poor financier.

4. Crowded writing. Letters in a word crowded, words also crowded; loops of one line running into loops above and below.

Denotes one with a narrow mind. One apt to worry too much about little things. Introspective and thoughtful.

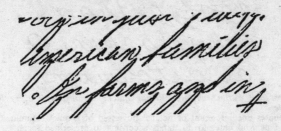

5. Letters compressed. Letters so close to each other that they seem to be lying on each other.

Denotes one given to economizing and saving; one apt to be avaricious.

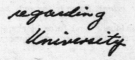

6. Diffused writing. Words and letters spread out unduly.

Denotes an extravagant nature. One with a superficial nature, hating hard work. Gets things done quickly. Lacks concentrative ability.

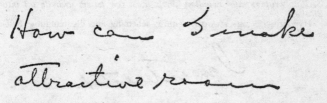

Speed

1. Fast writing. Writing streams along in continuous flow. No interruption in strokes.

Denotes a person with lots of energy and enthusiasm for things which claim his personal interest.

2. Slow writing. Writing is large and strokes are made surely indicating slowness of movement.

Denotes a person not inclined to take many chances or to do many things on his own initiative. One slow to make important decisions.

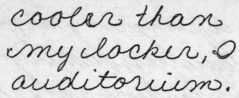

3. Fast and distinct writing. Writing quickly penned with every letter legible.

Denotes one intolerant of details; possessed of a quick, animated nature. One who hates to do things according to prescribed form.

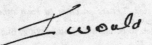

4. Fast and indistinct writing. Some letters only half-formed; occasional final letter left out.

Denotes strong individuality and force of character. Usually talented in some direction. Entertaining talker; ambitious; good imagination.

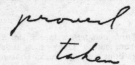

5. Fast writing, with dwindling finals. Last few letters dwindle off into stroke.

Hypocritical, untrustworthy nature; scheming and dissimulating. Self-willed.

Lines

1. Straight. Base line of writing is even; a ruler placed along the line of writing will help in determining the straightness of the line.

Denotes a sincere individual, straightforward in his actions and honest in his purposes.

2. *Ascending lines. Line of writing tends to rise.*
Denotes a lively, ambitious nature. One not easily discouraged; able to smile in the face of defeat.

...ding Simmons)
...kes voice at
...rd Conservatory

3. *Lines ascending then dropping.*
Denotes one with initial enthusiasm which peters out.

...p study . Also, what
would be available

4. *Lines ascending to unusual degree.*
Denotes a visionary, over-ambitious, impractical nature.

...camp for teen - age
concerts may be attended,
summer spots enjoyed?
On ..

5. *Lines descending then rising.*
Denotes one who has difficulty in getting started but once he has begun he finishes his task.

Thanking you for your

6. Series of ascending words.
   Denotes a nature given to careful consideration.

Any information you may

7. Series of descending words.
   Denotes an active, aggressive nature.

send me Your bulletin
& courses to be given

8. Descending lines.
   Denotes one lacking in ambition. One having a fretful and worrisome nature. Easily discouraged and suspicious of another's success. Moody disposition.

I have wanted
but unable to
about activities, c

9. Lines descending to a marked degree.
   Denotes one lacking in mental alertness. One in ill health.

I would like
in regard to

10. Last word in line droops.
Denotes one feeling low in spirits.

... and I am
ask if you have

Your signature—a distillation of your whole self

You write your name more often and with more concern and thought than any other words. You may write other words carefully or carelessly depending upon circumstances or upon the kind of a person you are, but your signature tends to take on a consistent or stylized form. Banks depend upon your writing your name the same way each time. Otherwise positive identification for check-cashing would be impossible.

Your signature is a perfect pen print in miniature of what a more complete sample of your handwriting would indicate. It can, however, be slightly inaccurate since most people write their names the way they like to be seen by others. There is also the possibility of your picturing yourself ahead of what you are striving to be as a person, if you still have not achieved your goal of individual accomplishment. But even if your signature may be an ideal, it does not necessarily mean that you are not as close to that ideal as you can ever be.

Signatures

1. Signature underlined.
Denotes a person with a forceful personality and having a healthy self-esteem.

Bob Hope

2. Signature larger in proportion to body of letter. (This rule holds true regardless of whether the letter is hand written or typewritten since it is the amount of paper space used for the signature that is the determining factor.)

Denotes one possessing a dominating personality.

- 5 -

de octubre, y aquel protocolo debe considerarse en la actualidad superado.

Estas son mis respuestas, querido Führer, a vuestras observaciones. Quiero con ellas disipar toda sombra de recelo y declarar mi entera, mi decidida disposición al lado vuestro, unido en un común destino histórico; del que desertar representaría mi suicidio y el de la Causa que yo he guiado y represento en España. No necesito ninguna confirmación en mi fe en el triunfo de vuestra Causa y me repito siempre leal seguidor de ella.

Creedme sincero amigo vuestro, con mi cordial saludo

3. Signature smaller in proportion to body of letter.
Denotes a self-centered individual. One who is reserved and self-conscious.

4. Period or dash after signature.
Denotes one accustomed to finishing what he starts.

5. Flourished signature.
   Denotes a person gifted in selling ideas to others. One with a promotional turn of mind.

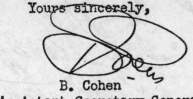

B. Cohen
Assistant Secretary-General
for Public Information

6. Middle initial included in signature.
   Denotes one possessing a proper sense of dignity.

7. Signature in backhand when the body of the letter leans forward.
   Denotes one appearing cold and unfriendly but is the reverse.

8. Signature leans forward when the body of the letter is in backhand.
   Denotes one outwardly ardent and loving, but inwardly less so.

9. Curved underscore under signature.
   Denotes one gracious of manner, adaptable, and capable of influencing others.

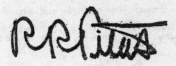

*10. One or more underscores under signature divided in half by two
short perpendicular lines.*
Denotes a person with commercial instincts.

11. Uniquely constructed signature.
Denotes a distinctive, original personality.

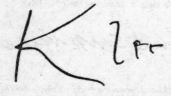

Paul Klee

Examine These Signatures for Style and Significance.

Compare your own signature with these famous historical personages
and see if any of them match your own. Maybe you are an undiscovered
genius!

Elbert Hubbard . . . his sound and original thinking earned for him the
title: "The Sage of East Aurora."

Nelson A. Rockefeller . . . his imaginative and bold approach to govern-
ment will make him long remembered as the Governor of New York State.

Walt Disney . . . this signature of Walt Disney is a design in itself and is so lively looking that it appears almost animated. If you have artistic talent it should show somewhat in your signature since your autograph is the real you in its purest form.

Emily Dickinson . . . a poetic personality whose handwriting mirrored the idealism and beauty of her soul as suggested by her haunting word-imagery. There is intuition in the broken letter forms and delicacy of spirit in the light-pressured script.

Walt Whitman . . . the "earthiness" of Walt Whitman's personality is indicated in strong-pressured and vibrant letter strokes of his handwriting. Such was the verse of this practical poet.

Robert Louis Stevenson . . . the author of *Treasure Island* and other books was a disciplined, detailed writer and his signature reflects these characteristics. It is heavy-pressured, carefully fashioned and incisively penned, indicating a penchant for perfection through sheer determination. He succeeded despite physical handicaps.

Walter Cronkite . . . CBS TV newscaster, is an individual known to millions. Mr. Cronkite is, of course, a clear thinker (connected letters, properly proportioned), has excellent judgment (even spacing between letters, between words and between lines) and he thinks along original lines (unique capital letters, especially the "W" in his signature). But he has a special characteristic: he is intellectually loquacious. We know this from his unusual combination of small letters with open a's and o's. Because of his insight and depth of thinking that we see in his carefully executed small letters, Mr. Cronkite is not only clear in his news reporting but also clever is his commentary.

A PARADE OF PRESIDENTS

What can you tell from their signatures?

1. George Washington

2. John Adams

3. Thomas Jefferson

4. James Madison

5. James Monroe

6. John Quincy Adams

7. Andrew Jackson

8. Martin Van Buren

9. William Henry Harrison

10. John Tyler

11. James Knox Polk

12. Zachary Taylor

13. Millard Fillmore

14. Franklin Pierce

15. James Buchanan

[signature: James Buchanan]

16. Abraham Lincoln

[signature: A. Lincoln]

17. Andrew Johnson

[signature: Andrew Johnson]

18. Ulysses Simpson Grant

[signature: U. S. Grant]

19. Rutherford Birchard Hayes

[signature: R B Hayes]

20. James Abram Garfield

[signature: J. A. Garfield]

21. Chester Alan Arthur

[signature: C. A. Arthur]

22. Grover Cleveland

[signature: Grover Cleveland]

23. Benjamin Harrison

[signature: Benjamin Harrison]

24. William McKinley

[signature: William McKinley]

25. Theodore Roosevelt

[signature: Theodore Roosevelt]

26. William Howard Taft

[signature: William Howard Taft]

27. Woodrow Wilson

[signature: Woodrow Wilson]

28. Warren Gamaliel Harding

[signature: Warren G. Harding]

29. Calvin Coolidge

[signature: Calvin Coolidge]

30. Herbert Clark Hoover

[signature: Herbert Hoover]

31. Franklin Delano Roosevelt

[signature: Franklin D. Roosevelt]

32. Harry S. Truman

Very sincerely yours,

[signature: Harry Truman]

33. Dwight D. Eisenhower

Dwight D. Eisenhower (signature)

Personality Sketches of Our Recent Presidents

John F. Kennedy (signature)

John F. Kennedy had a restless nature, which is mirrored in his swiftly-made signature. The late President was discerning and analytical (notice the angularity of his small letters) and he was very much alive with imagination; we know this from his tall, soaring capitals. The combination of boundless broadmindedness and an incisive awareness of the details that differentiate one pursuit or project from another, made him an ideal Presidential planner. Given time he would have completed projects that would have changed radically the course and pattern of American history. His forward-marching signature testifies to an energy drive motivated by strong inner purpose and fired by spiritual courage. There is no fear in the script of John F. Kennedy.

Lyndon B. Johnson (signature)

Lyndon B. Johnson possesses the handwriting of a born organizer and administrator. His script is connected, presenting a unified pen picture. The vertical hand signifies an individual who knows how to look at things objectively, to think before he goes into action. He has the discipline and self-control not to yield to emotional pressures.

His even pressure tells us that he believes in consistency of action, and his drawn-out ending strokes reveal an ability to bring projects to logical conclusions.

The combination of angular strokes with gracefully curved strokes reveals an unusually adaptive nature; a nature that responds just as efficiently to situations involving the emotions as to those involving purely intellectual stimulation.

Richard M. Nixon has a naturalness of manner which is reflected in his unaffected, clear script. There is dogged determination in Nixon's even-pressured handwriting. He exhibits a personality which will not undertake assignments that he knows he cannot accomplish. He fashions his capital letters plainly but not starkly which would suggest too practical a nature. His script is gracefully formed, with just the right amount of resilience in his strokes to indicate a nature quickly adaptable to changing situations and conditions.

He has an optimistic, friendly personality (note the medium-sized, forward-slanting script) and he will be the last one to plunge the nation into extravagances or excesses, either in domestic policies or in foreign affairs. We know this from his careful spacing, his conventional letter froms and his disciplined penmanship.

A Problem for Future Autograph Collectors

The "Autopen," a device which automatically writes a person's name "exactly" as he would write it, will pose a problem for all future autograph collectors if this signature-signing machine is adopted widely. Our most recent American Presidents have used this "imitation autograph" aid out of sheer necessity in order to handle expeditiously their extensive official correspondence and their document-signing.

The "Autopen" does a fairly accurate job of copying an individual's signature, but when the real signature is placed next to the copied version the difference is apparent.

To illustrate, here is Senator Robert Kennedy's "robot" signature and a facsimile of a letter to the author signed by Senator Kennedy, with a reference to his handwriting indicating that the signature is genuine.

Sincerely,

Robert F. Kennedy

Robert F. Kennedy

ROBERT F. KENNEDY
NEW YORK

United States Senate
WASHINGTON, D.C.

August 31, 1965

Mr. Robert Holder
P.O. Box 679
Chautauqua, New York

Dear Mr. Holder:

Thank you very much for sending me the issue of The Chautauquan Daily reporting my visit to the area. I had seen your account, and am pleased to have another copy of the story.

I can make little apology for my handwriting, except to say that it does occasionally suffer from my habit of signing mail while in transit.

With appreciation for your interest,

Sincerely,

Robert F. Kennedy

Robert F. Kennedy

Notice the greater strength of character (consistent, heavy pressure) and stability of personality (regularity of letter sizes) in the real signature.

As a further check of the authenticity of the signature of Senator Kennedy, included here is his autograph, below that of Senator Edward M. Kennedy, as it was written on the First Day Cover in memory of President John F. Kennedy. These signatures accompanied the first-day-of-issue envelopes using the five-cent John F. Kennedy memorial stamp.

Part 3

How handwriting can help you achieve more success and happiness

5. How parents can use handwriting

How to tell if your child is normal

The handwriting of a healthy, normal child will be written with a firm, even pressure, with not too much departure from the copybook style of writing he learned in school. Spacing may or may not be regular but this is not important since it only indicates more or less progress toward maturity and the exercise of adult, good judgment.

How to discover the child who is in conflict

The child who is not getting along well in school, who is not finding it easy to make friends, and the child who is a problem in his various environments—home, school, social, and so forth—mirrors his poor adjustment, his emotional conflicts, and his anti-social attitudes in his script. He cannot change his handwriting to hide his inner feelings or to throw people off the trail of discovery by deceit, misrepresentation, or by social withdrawal.

The picture of his troubles is plain in his writing. The value of handwriting analysis in this case is to aid the parent in arriving at the real cause of the child's unhappiness so that the cause may be understood and removed, if possible.

Poor marks in school may be due to a child's too short attention-span, that is, his inability to concentrate long enough on ideas to master them thoroughly. Handwriting which is replete with mistakes suggests mind-wandering. Small letters of varying sizes indicates inability to maintain a logical flow of thought. Slow writing is a sign of mental retardation or the necessity of hearing spoken ideas twice or more in order to comprehend them. The "slow reader" has received much publicity in recent months, but an equally important problem is the "slow hearer." So much of modern education reaches the child by way of oral expression that many a child is "lost" when a fast talker does the speaking.

Any disturbance in the rhythm or free-flow of a handwriting is a sure indication of conflict. If the writing lacks ending strokes, the child has fears of one sort or another. If the writing is cramped and compressed, combined with heavy pressure, he has anxieties related to some physical worry. Emotional trouble will be reflected in writing which tends to be vertical rather than forward, as it should be in the writing of most normal children.

14-year-old girl normally adjusted.

Conflict is beginning to show in this adolescent girl's writing.

This adolescent boy is really having trouble adjusting himself.

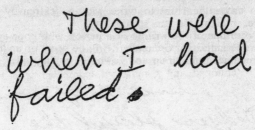

These were
when I had
failed.

This adolescent boy is coming out of his conflicts, but he still has much anxiety which he cannot help.

Understanding the slow reader

Lack of interest or lack of ability are two main causes of slow reading. If a child is not stimulated to want to enjoy his reading assignment he will be loath to start, careless about concentrating, and unconcerned about how fast he is supposed to be reading. For some children the mere fact that someone else wants them to read faster is not a sufficient reason for speeding up their efforts. Your child has no problem if it is simply a matter of insufficient interest in the reading matter. This is generally a temporary situation and he will be out of it before you know it.

When it is lack of ability that causes slow reading, the immediate question is: Lack of what kind of ability? If it is mental ability which is wanting then the slow reading is due to a difficulty in registering promptly the word changes on the page. Fast reading would only confuse in this case. Slow reading actually helps since it gives the child a chance to understand what he is reading.

Sometimes slow reading is caused by poor spelling knowledge so that the reader tends to stay with unfamiliar words longer than he should hoping that by thinking about them he will get their meaning.

If it is poor eyesight that slows a child's reading since it hurts his eyes to read, the solution to this problem is obvious. If the parent is negligent in this regard the school will usually find out about this type of physical flaw and do something about it.

If the slow reader has poor eyesight his handwriting will be awkward in formation, the small letters will be made large, the rhythm will be disturbed and jerky, and the pressure will be either very light or very heavy, depending on how poor the eyesight is. When sight is highly impaired it will tend to cause the child to write with an extremely heavy pressure.

The base line of the writing of a person with poor eyesight will never be straight. Generally it will be wavy or undulating and sometimes running up and down like rolling hills.

Since they won Dodgers played the this years

Poor eyesight resulting in slow reading.

When a slow thinker reads slowly, he reveals his sloweddown reactions by writing which is rounded rather than angular, tending toward the vertical rather than toward the slanted, with the formation of writing on the large side rather than on the small side, and by a completely unoriginal style of writing, fairly close to what he was first taught in school.

The poor speller has all the characteristics of the slow reader who reads slowly due to retarded mental activity. In addition, he shows sporadic heavy pressure in his writing where he is halted in his writing rhythm while he tries to figure out how to spell strange (to him) words.

To get a editor, look

Good eyesight but a slow thinker and a slow reader.

Help your child if he reads too fast

Children who read too fast miss out on important factual details which are necessary to learn in order to build up important stores of basic knowledge. Skimming is beneficial for certain types of reading material, but is actually detrimental in much school reading work where formulae, rules of English, historical concepts, and numerous assorted abstract ideas must be mastered.

Look at your child's handwriting to see if he reads too fast.

Speedy writing may be large or small. If it is large it will generally slant forward, have an even or light pressure, contain shaded strokes, be written with small a's and o's which are open at the top, and will be lacking in extra-ornamentation of any special sort. t-crossings will be lance-like, heavy at the beginning of the stroke and tapering at the conclusion. i-dots will be similarly made.

When fast writing is small the pressure will be medium or heavy, the slope will tend toward the vertical, the base line will be very straight and the capitals will be much larger than they should be in proportion to the small letters. t-crossings and i-dots will be firmly made.

Children who read fast can be taught to slow down, at least when it is necessary to absorb important ideas. Parents of these children will have no trouble in getting cooperation in this respect if they take the time to explain the situation to the children. This is because fast readers are highly intelligent and will use their intelligence to solve their problem of reading too fast after they realize it is interfering with their personal progress.

Juvenile Delinquency

How to foresee the juvenile delinquent

In any community, no matter how small, the number of adult-minded good citizens always outnumbers, by far, the number of child-minded youngsters heading down the dark path of juvenile misbehavior. If you are interested in cutting down the juvenile delinquency rate where you happen to be, you can examine the handwriting of the children you would like to know more about and you will discover quickly the reasons behind their behavior.

By knowing ahead of time what a child is *likely* to do you may be able to provide constructive alternatives to bad actions which will aid the individual to grow into a cooperative citizen.

Either slowed-up maturity or accelerated maturity may develop into anti-social action, since in both situations the child is not undergoing normal growth progress and feels out of place. Children who feel "out" tend to join "out" groups, and these are generally those gangs of individuals who plague the normal activities of people. Their main business seems to be to interfere with the normal functions of orderly society. This gives them a purpose, a sense of worth, and an opportunity to achieve.

Particularly dangerous is the juvenile who is more mature than his age group and who advances into adult forms of misbehaviour, dragging the less-than-normally mature children along with him. This type of delinquent will steal cars for joy rides, smoke, brag about his sex experiences (which may or may not be true, but his familiarity with the "right" terminology will enthrall the less-experienced and younger listeners), get drunk, talk back to law enforcement officers; in short, he will set the worst kind of bad example. He looks upon delinquency as a complete manifestation of manhood.

He comes from both poor and rich homes. In the poor home he may have been surrounded with adults who gave him his models for the bad behavior. (This is not always true, but true enough.) In the rich home the neglect of the parents may have forced him to make his own decisions more quickly than he should have, and having based them on childish foundations, he would naturally end up with warped actions.

In certain cases, when a child is adopted and there is no psychic connection between the parents and the stranger to the family, the child feels every neglect ten times more strongly and seeks satisfaction in a circle of friends outside the home. Too many times the circle proves to be of the wrong kind.

Extremely rounded and slow writing denotes the child who is maturing too slowly. Sharp angularity in writing of youngsters who are not out of high school together with dash-like dots and embellished capitals are all indications of a fast-maturing person who should be watched to make certain he gets the proper guidance at the time needed.

ghts went out way to school and it

Normal and gradual maturing.

t was even colder that they were

Maturing too fast.

Sex changes are part of the normal physical and psychic growth of a child through adolescence into adulthood. Some children experience more stress than others in this transition. There is a small percentage of youngsters who have excessively strong erotic tendencies during their growing-up period and, as a result, get into difficulties trying to satisfy them. If these children have to master self-control and the need for strengthening their will power as well as holding in check their extra sex urges, they will have to take it out on somebody. Generally, they take it out on Society.

Not all over-sexed boys and girls endeavor to find partners for their feelings in overt behavior, or even in sexual expression. If the child has a moral family background he may divert his energies into constructive channels totally unrelated to sex. If not, then the pursuit of physical release may lead him into unacceptable behavior. In all cases, however, there is always the problem of the excess energy which must be taken care of. If the organization of his social environment is such that the child cannot avoid boredom, he will seek stimulation and happiness in illicit or illegal gratification.

Excess sexual energy is indicated by writing which leans far forward, is written large with full upper and lower loop letters, is formed with a consistently heavy pressure but not necessarily muddy or pasty, and has a fairly straight base line. It must be remembered that this is not the writing of a perverted person but simply one who has an extra amount of what every normal person has in a fair amount.

Children can drift into delinquency

Because children must grow from immaturity into maturity, even the normal child can become delinquent if he is so weak-willed, unstable, and lacking in self-confidence that he will follow the lead of another in order to feel important and happy.

Light-pressured writing with weak t-crossings indicates indefinite will power. Varied slants to the lines of writing reflect the child's unstable attitude, and a roundness of the letter forms, especially the m's and n's, show the young person's susceptibility to the suggestions of others. These are the psychographological details that will warn the parent of the child who needs special adult guidance.

With this type of child often the mere knowledge that the parent is interested in his welfare and in the nature of his intimate friends, is enough to cause a constructive shift to the ideals of his own family situation and away from any destructive or anti-social ideas learned from bad juvenile associations. There is nothing "bad" in this kind of child but only the weaknesses inherent in a lack of knowledge and a lack of sufficient personally-powered determination.

The vicious delinquent and how to identify him

When juvenile delinquency takes a vicious turn there is real danger for all members of the community since any person of any age could be the victim. Newspapers contain daily reports of this kind of activity by teen-agers. Recently there was the case of some boys who hung live dogs in the basement of an apartment house. Parents were naturally concerned about what might happen to their small children if they met up with these crazed children. Children have been made into human torches and burned to death by young hoodlums whose only answer was, "We didn't know what we were doing."

Rapacious stabbings, brutal beatings, uncontrolled criminal assaults, and fires set by youngsters who care nothing for the lives they may endanger are the direct result of natures that are essentially sensuous, super-aggressive, and uncontrolled.

This much is general knowledge among doctors, psychiatrists, psychologists, teachers, clergymen, and other professional people constantly working with all sorts of personalities, from the sickest to the healthiest. But now the non-expert individual, especially the parent, can look at the handwriting of the child and satisfy himself concerning tendencies toward off-beat conduct.

Viciousness will indicate itself by extremely heavy pressure, muddy writing, slowly-drawn letter formations, inartistic letter forms, and punctuation which digs into the paper.

The silly bucket.

That had so long .

I dreamt that the

And when I awoke

Physical excesses (sexual, liquor, late hours), have begun to destroy the organization of this juvenile delinquent's personality, and his handwriting mirrors it perfectly. Note the hooks in the writing, indicating irritation with his environment; in this case it brands him as definitely anti-social, an attitude he could hardly help from having since the way of life he has chosen is so far from society's accepted code of conduct.

Keep a Handwriting History "Album" of Your Child

It will be helpful in understanding your child if you will keep a handwriting record of his "growing up" just as you enter photos in an album. Instead of preserving photos you will be saving periodic pen pictures of his personality, as it progressed or as it regressed. The usefulness of this writing chart of your child's character would be in the possibility of checking him before he contracted any personality quirks, and in helping him to get rid of unwanted habits.

The handwriting record would also give clues to his aptitudes along vocational lines early enough for you to assist him in getting valuable educational backgrounds.

Handwriting of some typical teen-agers . . . age 14

A lazy boy.

A shy boy.

A hard-working, intelligent girl.

An adolescent "rebel" (boy).

Morocco, and
and eastward,
— Algeria and Tunisia

A cooperative, friendly girl.

all lights
bad everyone.

A cooperative, friendly boy.

I reacted the
and found the

A poorly-adjusted boy.

can be called an
fertile area in an

A boy whose chief concerns are physical.

qualifications for
I am seventeen

A well-adjusted girl.

It was fun
happen again.

A girl revealing adolescent stresses and changes.

out at School. I
To school. When
arrives today.

*A boy with a speech defect coinciding with the halted rhythm
of his writing.*

In this movie
to smoke it were

A girl in the full flower of adolescent expression.

To the most wonderful
Mother
in
the
whole wide world!

Discovering hidden talents early

Parents are really perplexed when they try to discover what their children are best suited for vocationally. The constantly changing expressions of interest by the young people do not help the situation. Parents should remember that the apparent senseless shifting of interest from one type of work to another, often unrelated, is merely a part of growing up. It stems from the natural youthful desire to try out new things and to experiment.

There are some general ways to discover unobserved talents and leanings from looking at the handwriting of the child.

Mental interests

Size in handwriting is the quick key to whether or not your child has mental interests. Mental activity points to a strong possibility of success in college. Small, well-formed writing is a good indicator of mental alertness and concern.

Large writing is a sign that your child would be more apt to develop an interest in business or some other vocational pursuit not requiring assiduous college training.

If the writing is even-pressured as well as small, with the letters carefully formed, scientific aptitude is suggested.

Artistic talent

Artistic talent in a boy's or girl's script is indicated by original letter formations, especially the capital letters, and specifically the letters D and C.

Large writing.

a good question.

Small writing.

know the fundamentals

Artistic writing.

pertaining to
Cor teenagers

Mechanical interests

Plain, heavy-pressured writing, completely unoriginal, indicates a mechanical interest *in a child's writing*. If the letters are printed as well as plain, engineering aptitude is indicated.

Musical leanings

Rhythmic, smooth-flowing writing will indicate that your youngster would enjoy music, either as a hobby or as a vocation, depending upon the encouragement and opportunities for learning about music that come his way.

For further information

For actual aptitudes leading to vocational success, parents should read Chapter 8, "How Handwriting Can Help You Choose The Right Job." After a child has matured, through education and life experience, his interests, leanings, and special bents turn into definite talents and abilities. The age at which the change from mild interest to active aptitude for something takes place varies considerably from one child to another. Mozart showed his musical aptitude at an early age; your child may not reveal his liking for music until his high school days, when he decides to join the school orchestra.

Mechanical aptitude.

stay for the balance of

Musical aptitude.

If you could any information

Are your children college material?

The fond desire of a parent to send a youngster to college many times does more harm than good if the child is not college material. Graduation from high school is no guarantee of success in college. It is a cold fact that 50 per cent of those who begin university training do not complete it.

The wise parent would do well to study the handwriting of the student to search for a number of graphological signs generally found in the script of young people likely to enjoy and complete advanced training, such as college or other professional-type education.

Boys and girls who like to study, who have keen perceptions, and who know how to concentrate will have little trouble in finishing a college training program. If they have the additional merit of being consistent they will succeed with even the most difficult subjects.

Ability to concentrate is indicated by small writing, keen perception by angular letter formations, and consistency by letter forms in one line of writing appearing practically the same as letter forms in other lines of writing. Small letters need not all be the same size in this definition of consistency, otherwise it would rule out the "genius," the super-impressive type of person, and other unusual types of individuals who find college life exactly to their liking.

Good college material.

more detail on the additions. would make

How well are you helping your child grow up?

If you are over-disciplining your child so that he is afraid to strike out on his own, his handwriting will be slow and most letters will be well-formed.

If you are erratic in your discipline so that your offspring has to deal with extreme regulation on your part one day and excessive leniency the next day, then his writing will reflect your indecision by being incongruously constructed—with variable pressure, small letters of different sizes, and an uneven base line to the writing.

You can correct this situation by remembering that a certain amount of consistency is necessary in handling children. If you are consistent enough, then your child will write with only *some* of the small letters changing in size.

Ordinarily there is not too much danger in drastic discipline except when the child is highly creative and original. Then it may result in open rebellion. Firm pressure, original letter formations, and a tendency to small writing will point to the presence of a strong creative urge. It takes a clever set of parents to guide this type of child properly.

A girl growing up happily.

Well, that's just loads of ideas on

How is your child adjusting to life?

You can tell promptly if your child is making a happy adjustment to life in the inevitable unpleasant situations that do occur from time to time. If there are no hooks in the handwriting you can rest assured that all is well. If the script is replete with hooks and catches, then your child is meeting life with a built-in antagonism. You can help to blunt these unnecessary defense mechanisms by more attention and concern with his everyday activities. No child minds being made a fuss over. With some children the need for affection is so strong that they develop antagonisms if they are ignored in their basic need for love. Too young to get it outside the family, they turn to their parents from whom they rightfully expect it.

In summary

Handwriting analysis can easily help you as a parent to give more objective and more common sense guidance to your children. It will also keep you constantly aware of new developments in their character and personality.

In school relationships you will be able to come in closer psychological contact with your children's teachers, thus adding the full weight of your parental influence toward the better development and educational progress of your youngsters.

Watch your children's writing and you will be able to cut down considerably on the rest of your "watching."

6. How the businessman
can use handwriting

How to detect dishonesty before it really hurts

Dishonest action displays itself psychologically by stimulating worry and fear in the person who is catering to crookedness. Hence the handwriting of the dishonest individual will reveal symptoms of emotional upset and nervous tension. If you are suspicious of the trustworthiness of an employee, just watch his writing. If it suddenly seems more erratic than usual, more variable in pressure, and if the small letters constantly change in size, you have a dishonest person in the making. You cannot act too soon in removing temptation or in letting the worker go.

Picking out the petty pilferer

Many businessmen are concerned about the problem of pilfering. Large chain store operators write this off as part of their "shrinkage" loss, but to the small business operator this represents an important loss in profit that he would like to prevent. He cannot be his own private detective, so his next best action would be to check the handwriting of his employees to single out those responsible for goods stolen from the store or business.

The petty pilferer will usually write with an irregular base line, varying small letters, uneven pressure, simple letter forms, and will tend toward large writing with rounded m's and n's.

Psychologically, this type of person has the attitude that the world owes him a living. Therefore he feels free to take what he wants wherever he sees it. He does not consider that he is being dishonest.

The forger and how to detect him

Suppose you suspect some person in your business of forging your signature. How can you get some help in detecting him by studying his handwriting?

First, you must know how a forger operates. "Practice makes perfect" is his first rule of action. Before attempting to simulate a signature, the forger will practice making the signature he is going to imitate by "drawing" the details of the letters. After he has written the name scores of times so that he is sure of each individual letter form, he then copies the rhythm of the writer. In this way he prevents anyone from noticing possible breaks in the pattern of rhythm. Continuous, careful practice in forging the signature will result in a smooth, rhythmic, and authentic-looking signature.

So important is the rhythm in a signature that professional forgers turn the signature upside down and copy the writing pattern as they would a design. In this way they do not subconsciously allow their own handwriting rhythm to affect the writing they are imitating. If they did allow it to affect the rhythm it would also change the pressure, the i-dots, and other details which bank tellers can pick out quickly when checking names with bank signature record cards. The average person could be easily fooled with a hastily-forged name, but the forger is more interested in fooling the bank.

In finding the possible forger in your business, look for the person who has a smooth rhythm to his writing, angular letter formations (this indicates a keen mind), words which diminish in size denoting a suave and diplomatic nature, and writing which has a natural shading, that is, the pressure of the strokes is alternatingly thick and thin. Finally, look for capital letters which are *extremely* exaggerated and sweeping.

Unless the forgery in question is very crude you will find that the forger will write as indicated.

How the personnel manager can use handwriting analysis

The personnel manager can employ psychographology initially to screen and classify large groups of prospective workers. If aptitude tests are employed, the handwriting studies will aid in classifying persons for the various try-out aptitude examinations.

If a department store personnel manager has a hundred girls to interview for possible sales positions he could easily eliminate 75 per cent of the group because the handwriting would reveal quickly that most of them did not possess the needed talents to qualify for the selling jobs. He could not tell that from looking at them, but the handwriting would give him an "X-ray" insight revealing their real capabilities and natures. The time saved would be money saved for his organization. It is common knowledge among business people that too much time, energy, and money are wasted hiring unfit workers who have to be fired a short while after they have been taken on.

Psychographology can provide one more corroborating factor to substantiate previously arrived at conclusions concerning personnel, whether in the hiring phase or about workers already employed where accurate information is required for purposes of promotion or for other reasons. When one company buys another corporation, or when a banking organization is in the process of providing underwriting for a stock or bond issue of a company unfamiliar to them from the management angle, even a cursory examination of the writing of key personnel would bring out into the open important personality and character details of the people in question.

In any employer-employee relationship there are three "walls" which can be crumbled or pierced by handwriting study. The wall of definite deception, where an individual is trying to "put something over," can be broken through thereby bringing the situation in the open where it can be handled. For instance, if an employer suspects an employee of being malicious in his "slow-down" activity rather than just incapable of working faster, he can examine the worker's script for signs of a spiteful disposition.

The wall of indifference can be weakened. This is the trait in an employee which causes him to turn deaf ears to safety suggestions, pleas for company loyalty, and so forth. The handwriting of this type of person will be rounded in formation with simple letter forms. He can be reached and changed by being singled out for special classroom instruction and indoctrination. As it works today, industrialists educate everybody when they could save money by concentrating on the few who need the information most. They are the "accident-prone" and the poor cooperators.

The wall of misunderstanding can be leveled by having a record of the proper personality-picture of each employee noted on his personnel card, and then using that knowledge to clear up the mental fog resulting from human stress of one sort or another. Human relations can be smoothed tremendously once some central person, such as the personnel manager, has a dependable tool to help him in straightening out plant or office difficulties. Handwriting analysis can be that tool.

The personnel manager can use handwriting analysis as a kind of "Geiger counter" to discover hidden talents in modest-minded people who naturally would not be advertising their particular capabilities. This sort of program of personality exploration could be carried on without the knowledge of the workers concerned since all that would be needed would be the specimens of handwriting available on the personnel record blanks.

Potential trouble-makers could be discovered before they were hired, morons would be seen immediately for what they were, "queer" applicants could be quickly passed by, and those with top-talent personalities could be given positions more in line with their abilities rather than the conventional "start-at-the-bottom" procedure employed by many firms. A "race-horse" temperament gains little by being relegated to work-horse duties. It must be remembered that much opposition to present-day conventions in promotion and job progress comes from those who are anxious to protect their own personal job interests, with no regard for the over-all benefits of the company.

The logical thinker is best for business

In the world of business and finance you must plan the end before you ever begin a project or underwrite an experiment. You must also be familiar with background, history, and be able to keep in mind all kinds of important facts bearing upon the ever-changing condition of the economic and social environment in which you, as a businessman, will function daily.

This takes a steady thinker, a logical mind, and an individual who can keep on the subject—who can proceed logically and regularly from step one to step two, and a person who can complete what he starts. If you are fitted for business, that is, for business success, your letters will be connected in the words, your writing will slant forward, it will be penned with heavy pressure, and will tend toward small size script.

Stay out of business if you live by hunches. People who are guided by intuition and do not follow the dictates of their reason show it in handwriting which is equally illogical and disconnected. Many of the small letters will not be attached to the others in the words. The more disconnection in the writing, the more illogical the writer. Pressure generally varies from heavy to light in the writing of the truly intuitive person suggesting that there is some kind of emotional cause of the lack of logic.

Watch out for the wasters

Nobody loves a time-waster, but businessmen are especially sensitive on this score. Time-wasters write large and use extra flourishes and embellishments in their writing.

Motion-wasters, people who take three or four steps when one or two would do, generally write a large hand.

Accident-prone people

Accident-prone people lack good muscular coordination and reveal this characteristic by writing which is lacking in *word rhythm*. The pressure of the writing is light or uneven and the punctuation is careless.

Persons who do not mind monotony

Businessmen who need to hire workers for monotonous or repetitive tasks would find it profitable to hire people who can stand the sameness of a job without becoming unhappy about it and then quitting. Constant hiring and firing is expensive to any employer, whether he has a work force of two or a thousand.

People who can stand monotonous work write a simple hand, have a script entirely lacking in originality, and make all small letters the same size. The handwriting will never be small and never heavy-pressured.

Time-waster.

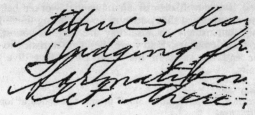

Accident-prone person.

like to attend

Able to stand monotony.

When you hire

Almost anyone can hide faults of character and weaknesses of personality while in the brief process of being hired. It is only after a job is secured that these faults emerge and cause concern on the part of the unlucky employer. In order that undesirable workers will not be hired, consult the following list of commendable characteristics with their accompanying graphological signs. Hire only those individuals who have one or more of these traits of character, and who are health and hence happy-minded.

1. *Healthy*
Even-pressured writing. Rhythmic style of hand. Shaded down-strokes.
2. *Tactful*
Writing never large. First letter of word larger than rest of word. a and o closed.
3. *Open-minded*
Words well-spaced in relation to each other.
4. *Reliable*
Straight lines of writing. Small letters all same size.
5. *Cooperative*
Small m and n made with sharp tops. Capital letters not more than three times as tall as small letters.
6. *Even-tempered*
t-crossing made with sure, straight stroke. Same pressure throughout writing.

When you fire!

If you are the "boss" you will occasionally have the unpleasant duty of firing an employee. Time and trouble will be saved if you will dismiss an unwanted worker before he does the drastic deed that puts him on the "firing line." People are dismissed usually because they are lazy, dishonest, careless, or troublemakers. Below are the characteristics to watch out for and the signs in the handwriting that divulge the bad traits.

1. *Lazy*
Slow writing. Rounded hand. Small m and n rounded at top.

2. *Dishonest*
Irregular lines of writing. Wavy baseline. Small letters a, o, d, g, open at bottom. Small letters of different sizes.

3. *Careless* (*Slovenly, low-standard work*)
Careless punctuation. t-bars and i-dots occasionally left out. Uneven, straggling writing. Margin at left uneven.

4. *Troublemaker* (*mean, spiteful*)
Absence of ornamentation in writing. Heavy pressure. Vertical or backhand writing. Lower point of small p made sharp with return stroke to right of stem. t-bar heavy and club-shaped. Small m and n pointed at top.

(These two specimens were written by individuals holding exactly the same type of job but working a thousand miles apart. Note the similarity. The job required only mediocre ability. Otherwise their laziness and carelessness would not have been tolerated.)

Whom should you promote?

The problem of whom to promote arises often in the average business concern. Simply because an individual makes good at his job is not a sure-fire guarantee that a more important position will be filled equally well. Some people perform poorly if given too much responsibility, in fact, will frequently refuse advancement if they can do so without giving offense. Hence, it would be of great value to know ahead of time who would be most likely to welcome the shouldering of increased responsibility. Only people possessing real *executive ability* function profitably for all concerned when promoted to a higher and more responsible position.

Signs of *EXECUTIVE ABILITY*

Signature constructed with speedy movement. Strong pressure. Vertical or forward slant to writing. Large capitals and small small letters. Individually styled writing.

Robert W. Sarnoff
President

A Famous Executive.

How to select a good salesman

Businessmen lose more time and money hiring and firing sales people than they would like to admit. Here are five characteristics which make for a superior sales personality, and the handwriting signs that he should possess.

1. *Healthy Enthusiasm*
Hurried writing. Down strokes shaded. Writing never small.

2. *Pleasant Persistence*
Small y and g often ending in strokes instead of loops.

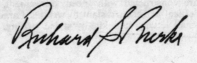

3. *Clear Thinking*
Strokes and loops of one line clearly separated from lines above and below.

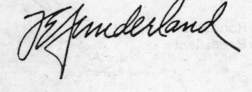

4. *Fluent Talker*
Small d and t looped. Small a and o open at top.

5. *Optimistic Approach*
Ascending lines of writing. Down strokes firm.

Summary

Graphology is an instant aid for the businessman, whether he runs a simple store or directs a giant corporation. He must operate at a profit if he is to remain in business.

Everything the businessman needs to know about people is revealed in their handwriting. Dishonesty can be detected, forgery can be uncovered, pilfering can be stopped before it starts, and just the right kind of people for jobs can be selected by studying the writing of job applicants.

There is no need of hiring time- and material-wasters or accident-prone people. Hiring and firing can be done efficiently and with a great saving of money if handwriting is looked at to round out the worker's personality picture.

7. How the teacher can use handwriting

As a teacher you can get a clear picture of yourself so that you can present your personality best to your students. Examining the writing of your teaching associates and that of your principal will give you the necessary "inside information" about their characters so that you will be able to work with them smoothly and happily. You won't have to know their family history to find a basis for understanding. It will be enough to get a glimpse of what your professional friends are like from looking at their writing.

Reducing unpleasant personal impacts

If you are a strait-laced teacher (look for fairly-perfect, conventional letter forms and even pressure in your script), apt to be shocked easily—and visibly—by certain student conduct or tales of misdeeds, you should refrain from exhibiting consternation when you run into these situations. This will keep the pupils coming to you with their confidences and provide an open channel for guidance, educational and otherwise.

Cramped letter forms will classify you as narrow in your thinking. Students will like you better if you enlarge your interests, which is always possible, even if you cannot change overnight from a staid individual to one exuding broadmindedness.

If you dot your i's with a meticulous round dot, you need to develop a more spontaneous and reactive sense of humor. It is not enough for you to "smile inside" when something funny happens in class; your students need to know that you have a good sense of humor. With children, "seeing is believing."

*With kindest regards   awhile & I
                          with him.*

much if you

information

shirk the duties

Expanding your personality will make it easier to be democratic rather than dictatorial in your student contacts, and
will assist you in penetrating into the personality of each
child. The better your emotional relationship with the learner,
the better your teaching. Students find it easy to remember
what you say when they like you.

Watch your will. If you cross your t's with a light and
almost pressureless bar, you are not presenting yourself to
your class as a challenging person. You may have the best
of precepts, you may be a moral and spiritual ideal, and you
may know all the right answers, but unless you take a stand
in your classroom you will be interesting but never inspira-
tional. As a teacher you should set an example, of course,
but a lively, working model type of human that children can
be challenged into copying. So depart from your wishy-washy
approach to life and let your youngsters know what you
believe about life, the good life, the proper life, and the kind
of living that builds the happy and worthwhile citizen.

Observing adolescent changes

When a teacher becomes alarmed because an otherwise
diligent thirteen- or fourteen-year-old suddenly develops a
lazy, "don't care" streak, a glance at the handwriting of the
adolescent will reveal that important physical changes are
taking place, disturbing the child's growth rhythm, and likewise affecting the writing. Well-formed letters will turn into
letters of all shapes and sizes, with the formerly straight lines
of writing starting to waver and take uncalled-for tangents.
What has happened is that the physical changes are being
reflected in the upsetting of the nervous system, which in
turn disturbs the smooth flow of the writing movement. Sharp

"digs" of pressure will also be apparent in the writing of the adolescent when change is taking place.

The understanding teacher will take this reversal of character in his stride and wait for the adolescent to regain his emotional balance, a process which does not occur overnight but may take weeks. He must realize that adolescent physical disturbances interfere with concentration, reduce the desire for mental pursuits, and cause the child to be over-concerned with physical interests. There may actually be minor teen-age rebellion if the teacher attempts to be extra-strict at this time. Hence the wisest policy is to continue to keep up the classroom standards of work but to relax any evident tensions through shorter and less-intensified work periods.

If a teacher has trouble with adolescent boys it is generally because they are slower in passing through adolescence, thus making the "upset" period more or less permanent for the year's course. The writing of boys who are adjusting themselves easily to adolescence will be fairly regular and approaching angularity in form.

Handling discipline cases

If a teacher knows in advance what a student's personality is like, he can handle him easier and with more confidence when an emergency develops, such as a serious infraction of school or classroom discipline.

A girl or boy who "talks back" to a teacher will be better understood if the reason for the impudent speech is known. For instance, if a student speaks rudely because he is quick-tempered, it might be assumed that he is not being as personal in his remarks as would a person having a "slow fuse" temper, who would be more insulting and deliberate.

The quick-tempered boy or girl will cross t's with a lance-like stroke and will write a fast, forward-slanting hand. The person slow to anger will cross his t's with a short, even-pressured stroke and will tend toward vertical or backhand writing.

Discovering the cooperators

In seating children in class it is often a simple matter to solve a "problem student" situation—one who cannot keep quiet—by surrounding him with more cooperative youngsters. If this can be accomplished at the start of the term, it will solve the problem for the year. The trick is in picking out the cooperative children early.

You can find the cooperators in your class by looking for the following features in their handwriting: even pressure, letters made mostly all the same size, forward slanting script, and capital letters not too original in formation.

You do not have to examine handwriting to discover the noncooperators. They will make themselves known.

dark. I reacted other students

Pressure "digs" indicating adolescent change.

14 years old that

Hot-tempered.

As I approached told me to go

Slow to anger.

until future were to be given.

Cooperator.

Understanding and building on individual differences

One of the perplexing problems in education today is recognizing and working constructively on the individual variances in the children in the classroom. The efficiency of mass education is directly related to how personalized each lesson can be.

Once a teacher has the correct picture of the personality of a child as he sees it mirrored in his handwriting, he can adjust his teaching accordingly. Few teachers are so skilled in diagnosing personality patterns that they can classify children by mere association in a school situation. There are too many "special" cases, and often they are not "extremes," such as "gifted" or "stupid," if we can use such terms.

The shy child may be repressed

No teacher should assume that because a child is quiet and attentive that he is necessarily developing normally under his teaching. He may have little readiness for learning by being in a state of unhappiness brought about by suppression at home. He will be polite and cooperative as a "cover-up" for his feeling of inferiority. This type of child should be given many opportunities to express himself, to lead, to mix with other classmates in committee work, and otherwise to approach normal expressive activity, the right of every youngster in a schoolroom. How do you recognize him from his writing? He will write contracted letter forms, generally small writing, light-pressured t-crossings and i-dots, ending strokes will be short, the style of writing will be conventional. It will be written vertical or backhand.

had some experience as a
I hold and get many

Notice the contractive signs in this shy person's writing.

I would like to

In contrast, observe the natural and expansive quality of this person's writing. Her parents have allowed her full and free expression.

Helping the emotionally disturbed child to avoid accidents

Even among adults, when emotions get out of hand so that the individual is more concerned about the way he feels than about where he is going or what he is doing, accidents are bound to happen. Emotional storms make anyone careless and thoughtless, but when children become angry, fearful, strongly jealous, or "bothered" in certain ways, their chance to escape injury or death from an accident drops dramatically.

Each year some 12,000 children die from accidents, many emotionally induced. In fact, accidents are the chief cause of death among children up to age 14.

The natural awkwardness coincident with growing up becomes an additional handicap when the youngster meets an emergency situation and needs every bit of physical and mental coordination to avoid an accident. So when he is emotionally upset he has another strike against him.

The teacher can watch for signs in handwriting of emotions which are disturbing the child and can use the power and persuasion of his personality to help the child weather the emotional storm. Each situation will be different, but the general over-all approach will be the same: the cause of the upset must be sought out and either removed or explained so that the child has a fair chance to achieve emotional balance.

Emotional imbalance shows in writing which is badly spaced, wavy lines of writing, small letters varying in size, assorted t-crossings, uneven pressure, and a tendency toward illegibility.

Detecting nearsightedness

If a child is not keeping up with his classmates, his failure to achieve might be due to nearsightedness, one of the most prevalent of eye defects. If his parents have not discovered the eye weakness, he may be hiding his handicap by guessing at words he cannot see on the blackboard, thus missing out on that important part of the teaching and learning processes.

The teacher who is ever alert to the tell-tale signs in a person's writing will be able to spot the nearsighted child by the uneven lines of his writing and by the fact that the youngster so afflicted will begin each line of writing so that it slants at a different angle from the one before it.

Naturally, the nearsighted child will have a reading difficulty because he will have to hold his book close to his eyes, increasing nerve tension as well as eye strain and leading to quicker fatigue. Social and emotional maladjustment may develop in the nearsighted pupil since he is not clearly aware of what is going on immediately around him. This generates fear and irritability.

The teacher can help the situation by placing the nearsighted child as near to the blackboard as possible and then passing on the health data to the proper school authorities for further investigation and possible contact with the parents regarding corrective measures.

Other observable signs of nearsightedness include frequent eye-rubbing, persistent inattention, and squinting at material he has to read in class.

She thurned on had to look for nothing to do. ~~could~~ couldn't we looked

Checking marks

Often a teacher will want to know how his marks or grades check with the actual ability of a child. In other words, is a student working up to his normal capacity?

Generally speaking, the larger the writing the less scholastic ability, and the smaller the writing the more mental activity of the boy or girl in question. There is one important caution. Sometimes a student who has an excellent memory will write large yet will earn good marks. In this case, the large writing is always rather original in formation. This type of student does not think things through but memorizes great quantities of *facts* and uses this information to pass tests, answer questions in class, and write what appear to be highly logical compositions. He will have a difficult time in college when he has to think for himself and develop original ideas.

Discount handwriting scales

Handwriting scales should not be used in judging the writing accomplishments of students since there is a subconscious compulsion by you, as the teacher, to classify "good" writers as better than "poor" writers, especially if you have never put any credence in graphological indications. This foolishly puts a premium on mediocrity.

Actually, the more the variation from the normal or average legible writing, the more the individual is using his intelligence, whether for good or bad. Unless he is a criminal, the fair presumption is that he is employing his brain power for constructive purposes.

Summary

As a teacher today you cannot know too much, either about yourself or about those around you in your school. Handwriting study will tell you what you are really like so that you can improve your personality to the point where it makes your teaching more efficient and your students happier.

Knowing your pupils better through analyzing their script will give you new skill in smoothing over rough spots, and in helping them in their handicaps.

All the things you are expected to do as a modern-day teacher will not seem so impossible when you know you can use handwriting revelations as an aid to your educational and personal understanding.

8. How handwriting can help you choose the right job

Setting the stage

Several years ago the head of a large publishing concern called me into his office and startled me with this statement:

"I want you to help us select a new sales manager for our Canadian territory."

I sank back into my chair waiting for his next words.

"Here are samples of the handwriting of four of our best Canadian salesmen. Tell us which one you would recommend for the job of sales manager."

I spread the scripts out before me, carefully examining the peculiarities of each handwriting specimen.

"You can eliminate this man," I began. "He would go all to pieces if he were given additional responsibility."

"That's strange," my friend exclaimed. "He has the best sales record of the four people you are analyzing."

"As a salesman he is very successful," I explained. "He has the required enthusiasm, interest in others, and high intelligence, qualities necessary for success in selling. However, you are asking me to select an *executive,* and he is definitely too loosely organized to serve well in that capacity."

"Your point is well taken."

I held up the second sample of handwriting and continued:

"You won't want this person to direct your sales activities, either. He is too unreliable. Not dishonest, necessarily, but the variation in the size of his small letters, the uncertain t-crossings, and the wavy base line all indicate a vacillating character. You would never be sure of just what this person was doing. You want a man as sales manager who can make decisions and stick by them."

"We are down to two choices. I hope you don't eliminate both of them."

"I may have to, unless you want me to select the best of the lot."

147

"To tell the truth, this is a sort of an emergency and I will have to give the job to one of these four men, at least temporarily."

"Well, let's look at this one," I remarked, selecting one of the two remaining samples.

"Oh, that's Charlie's. He's . . ."

"Don't tell me anything at all about him," I broke in. "It will make my analysis more objective. I don't want to be influenced by anything but the writing I see here."

My friend agreed and asked me to go on.

"If you want a sales manager who can make everybody happy, one who will run up large entertainment bills, and a person who will hog all the big accounts for himself, here is your man."

"That is just what we do not want," said my client. "We want an executive who knows how to supervise the work of others, a man who knows how to sell but who can make more money for us by helping the salesmen under him increase sales in their territories. If this fellow is the 'glad hand,' and the 'I'll take all the credit,' type, we might as well eliminate him, too."

"That leaves us one more, but don't get worried," I said, smiling. "I saved this one for last because he is the man you should select for your new sales manager. Most signs in his handwriting show him to be fitted for the position."

"What, for instance?" queried my interested friend.

"Notice the speedy way his signature is written. That's a good sign of executive ability. Observe the straight base line, the consistency of the letter forms, and the even pressure, all signs of reliability. His lofty capitals indicate imagination; he will never whine and complain that there is no more business in his territory. His angular letter forms show adaptability and an ability to get along well with others. He . . ."

"Pardon me for interrupting you," my client remarked, "but I think you will be interested to know that this is also the man I have chosen for the job. I called you in just to make sure I had made the right selection."

Several months later I received a phone call from this man to the effect that the applicant I had recommended for the position of sales manager was doing one of the best jobs of sales direction ever experienced by the company.

Are you in the right job?

Just because you are paid well and you work hard does not necessarily mean that you are in the right job, *for you.*

It might be the right job for your employer who gets the advantage of your plugger-type personality, but it may be that you are unhappy and would profit personally by a change.

Everybody has special aptitudes for work which they can do better than other kinds. If you have a strong feeling of frustration about your job, it may well be that you have to exert yourself too much to achieve expected results. There must be some other type of work for which you have a greater aptitude. Take a look at your hobby. It may be a key to what you would enjoy doing as a life work. Now look at your handwriting to make an objective test.

Some Handwriting Helps to Check Your Job Aptitudes

Creative ability

Creative ability is indicated in original letter forms. Artists, designers, photographers, architects, window dressers, writers, and inventors cannot be successful without this talent.

These Are Airplane Builders

Notice the feeling of flight and movement that is apparent in these specimens of the handwriting of representative airplane builders. It is almost as if the wind were sweeping back over the letters in the signatures.

All of the illustrated names signify imagination, energy, determination, clearness of thought, and the ability to create new entities from assembled details.

Sincerely,

[signature: Lawrence D. Bell]

President
Bell Aircraft Corp.

[signature: Harold W. Douglas]

PRESIDENT DOUGLAS AIRCRAFT COMPANY, INC.

[signature]

Vice-President in Charge
Airplane Division, Curtiss-Wright Corporation

These Are Authors

Here are the signatures of some of the literary great. There isn't a conventionally-formed autograph in the lot!

[signatures: Zane Grey, J Masefield, Edna Ferber, Robert Frost, John Buchan, G.K. Chesterton, and another]

[Willa Cather]

[Robt. P. Tristram Coffin]

[Joseph C. Lincoln]

[Franklin Kane]

[Hugh Walpole]

Carl Sandburg

[Eugene O'Neill]

[Cornelia Otis Skinner]

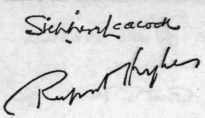

Helen Gurley Brown, Editor of "Cosmopolitan"

Here is the handwriting of today's "modern woman," Helen Gurley Brown, Editor of *Cosmopolitan* magazine. The script is firm-pressured, indicating energy that is under control—and the rhythm pattern is swift and energetic, denoting an enthusiasm for living. The line of writing rises, reflecting optimism, and the letter-forms are plain and unaffected, suggesting that her interests are practical, seldom for show. Because she is determined and resolute (we see this in the great number of horizontal strokes) she sometimes gives the impression of being more insistent than she really is. Her vitality and enthusiasm act to project her personality so that she stands out among others.

One would expect her script to reflect a strong degree of masculinity and more than a normal amount of aggressiveness, since Miss Brown is succeeding magnificently in what women often call a man's world. However, she is distinctly feminine. Notice her many rounded m's and n's, revealing a pliable rather than an inflexible nature. Observe, too, that her handwriting slants to the right, a sign of an affectionate nature. The fact that she signs her name in a vertical, reserved manner when the main body of her script slopes to the right indicates that she has a subconscious desire to appear to the world as one who can hold her emotions in check, to cope objectively with a competitive business environment.

Her romantic nature is signified in the underscores, the extra periods and the use of the exclamation point. She shows scope and breadth of mind plus excellent judgment by the wide spacing between words and lines. Her sense of organization and her executive ability are revealed in the careful punctuation and the pressure-emphasis on her final strokes. Occasional broken word formations tell us that she has her womanly flashes of intuition, giving her a special advantage over people chained to logical thinking. Here we see her insight and creativity.

Miss Brown has transcribed a pen picture of one who is making the most of her natural attributes!

*Cosmopolitan is a magazine
for girls between the ages of 18 and 34 —
they have a job — are good citizens —
pay their bills — they adore men
but they don't live through a man....
they're busy doing it themselves !
They want some of the power, some
of the glory, some of the love and
recognition and many that come
from making a contribution to
the world.*

Helen Gurley Brown

Fluency of thought

Fluency of thought is needed by those who desire to teach, to become lawyers, to sell, to supervise others, or to work at jobs where ideas must be communicated clearly and often. Forward-slanting, angular writing, written fast reveals this aptitude.

*the above-
particular,*

Visual memory

Visual memory, an aptitude needed in business pursuits particularly, although this talent is useful in the upper echelon of all types of work activity, is indicated by heavy pressured writing, even if the heaviness is not continuous. Sporadic increases in pressure tell us that the writer has visual memory but needs to prod himself to remember what he sees.

Natural beauties .
I would appreciate

Musical aptitude

Musical aptitude is seen in smooth-flowing, rhythmic writing. If the writing is heavy-pressured and original as well as rhythmic, there is also present the aptitude for composing music.

taken piano
s. I prefer private

Aptitude for details

Aptitude for details is necessary for scientists, engineers, college professors, librarians, editors, researchers, and similar workers. Small, firm-pressured writing indicates an aptitude for details.

will not be able
the photography for the

Capacity for working independently

Aptitude for independent activity is shown by writing which is vertical or backhand. The smaller the writing, in combination with the vertical hand, the greater the capacity for working alone is possessed by this type of person.

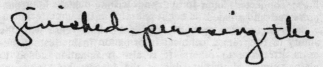

Number sense aptitude

Number sense aptitude is needed by cashiers, checkers, warehouse clerks, tool crib workers, and stock room employees. This special bent is indicated by writing which contains letters which look like numbers, such as a g made like a figure 8, y stem which appears like an l, and o's which are almost like perfect circles.

Persons with superior number sense, with proper professional training, can succeed as accountants, actuaries, statisticians, mathematicians, physicists, and similar occupations.

Handwriting of Louis Hausman, Vice President of CBS Radio.

Sales talent

Selling aptitude in its lowest form is indicated in handwriting which is written medium or large and which slants to the right. The friendly, expressive person can succeed in simple selling situations, such as counter sales in department stores.

Sales-demonstration aptitude requires a knowledge of spatial relations, logical thinking, and some feeling for the dramatic. Hence, to the forward slant there must be added these additional signs: even spacing of words, letters, and lines; connected letter-forms, and writing which is strong-pressured and shaded.

Sales-engineering aptitude combines selling sense with the ability to re-arrange technical information in interesting patterns attractive to others. It is also imagination added to plain selling. Naturally, this is the highest kind and the hardest type of selling.

The handwriting of the person with sales-engineering aptitude will slant forward, contain large and originally formed capitals, be written with speed, have an angular form to the small letters, stream along with firm and even pressure, and will tend toward small writing. The smaller and more detailed the script, the greater the mastery of technical or scientific details and thus the more effective the sales talent of the person.

John F Conn

J H Kindelberg

King Li Coul

Supervisory capacity

Supervising aptitude, or the skill of being able to direct the activities of others, involves emotional control and the ability to look at life objectively. Emotional coloring must be drained from disrupted situations so as to win the confidence of the people being supervised.

The good foreman or supervisor will write a medium or large hand, will use a forward slant, maintain fairly even pressure, cross his t's with a strong stroke, make his capitals plain and unadorned, and will space his writing so that it is well-separated.

Leadership qualities

Aptitude for leadership is closely related to the desire to improve a situation by adding the force of your personality to it. People who lead are generally accepted because they help the nonleaders to get somewhere, and in doing so tend to improve a situation. Hence, leaders are organizers, able to coordinate other people's different personalities, individuals with vision, and persons forceful in their character. Leadership can be good or bad. Good leaders will attain their ends without destroying the personal worth of their followers.

A good leader will write a strong-pressured hand, capital letters will be full and rounded, letter forms will be angular, some words will be connected, writing will never be backhand, and letters and words will be well-spaced.

Promotional and merchandising sense

Promotional and merchandising sense is easily noted in handwriting by the presence of unusually large and sweeping capitals, coupled with medium or large small letters, well-spaced, with the entire pattern of writing accomplishing a definite "effect."

Aptitude for dramatics

An aptitude for dramatics is observed in script which is firm-pressured combined with natural shading, an "open" appearance to the writing, and simple letter formations tending toward large writing.

John Galsworthy

Ability to work smoothly with people

An aptitude for working smoothly with others is seen in handwriting which is angular, smooth-flowing, and tending toward small writing but never tiny. Capital letters are never larger than necessary to harmonize with the rest of the script.

Sampson R. Field

Summary

Handwriting can help you select the right job. The secret is in your script. Just study it. It will indicate what your aptitudes are, what you can do best, and easiest. Then change to the job that brings out the best in you, and the position that pays you for what you can do better than most other people.

If you are the leader type, your handwriting will tell you. Look at the way you write and then go the way you should go. It will be pleasanter that way.

Remember, you may be wasting your God-given talents, and making yourself unhappy in the bargain. Turn that vocational corner now. You may help yourself to some delightful dividends.

9. How handwriting can help
you find more happiness
in marriage

Understanding each other

People considering marriage or persons already married should read this book together. It is necessary that two individuals planning to live together as man and wife should know as much about each other's real character and personality as possible at an early date.

To wait until experience has revealed this information to each other is a tragic waste of time because it is possible to shorten this learning period considerably by scientific observations of each other's handwriting.

Complete compatibility makes the best marriage

There are many reasons why two people become attracted to each other enough to get married, but if they are not compatible the marriage will either be an unhappy one or will end in divorce. Incompatibility or lack of harmony helps fan little fires of antagonism and irritation which cut across the whole of life. Sparks fly when the unfriendly personalities clash in unpreventable friction.

The handwriting of truly compatible people will be remarkably similar, since their basic character make-up will be essentially the same. The only differences will be due to special traits which belong to the male or to the female For instance, both parties may write a forward-slanting large hand, but the woman will write with a much lighter pressure than will the man, in most cases, since she will be expressing her femininity by indicating less insistence of nature (a masculine trait).

If all men were men and all women were women, the theory of opposites attracting each other would work out perfectly and there would be no unsuccessful marriages. But each individual possesses masculinity or femininity only to a degree. The greater the drift from your basic sex, the slimmer will be your chances for true marriage compatibility. Before picking a marriage partner, find out the extent of his sex purity and then match it with your own sex consistency. This can all be done easily by studying the handwriting for signs of masculinity and for features of femininity.

Are you more masculine or feminine?

The fact that no person is 100 per cent masculine or 100 per cent feminine is the reason you cannot distinguish accurately the sex of a writer from his handwriting. Each personality is a bundle of traits and the nature of these traits, whether they be masculine or feminine ones, determines the extent of your sex. Some women have so many masculine characteristics that they are labeled "mannish"; on the other hand, some men are decidedly of a feminine nature, because of the predominance of feminine traits in their make-up.

Following you will find a list of masculine and feminine traits with the signifying graphological signs. Study your handwriting and classify yourself. You must rate 75 per cent in one column or the other to be the man or woman you think you are!

Masculine

Trait	Sign
1. Aggressive.	1. Angular, heavy writing; p made with lower point sharp and upstroke on right of stem; t-bar heavy.
2. Impatient.	2. Letters begin with straight, inflexible stroke; finals point downward; fast writing; t-bar dashed to right of stem.
3. Speculative.	3. Badly spaced writing; loops of one line running into loops of line above and below.
4. Adventurous.	4. Letters hurriedly written; large capital letters in forward slanting writing.
5. Believes in his sex.	5. No graphological sign.
6. Fighting instinct.	6. Heavy, coarse writing; letters begin with straight, inflexible stroke; p made with lower point sharp and upstroke at right of stem; letters never cramped.
7. Desires on sight.	7. Shaded cross strokes; hasty writing.
8. Material-minded.	8. Heavy writing with finals turned down.

Trait	Sign
9. Vain and ambitious.	9. Very high capitals; hasty writing, with cross strokes, t-bar, and line of writing slanting upward.
10. Jealous and possessive.	10. Forward slant to writing; letters hurriedly made; terminal strokes dwindling to the right.

Feminine

Trait	Sign
1. Passive.	1. Rounded writing in vertical or right slant.
2. Patient.	2. Neat, uniform, small writing; initial strokes absent.
3. Cautious.	3. Capital D closed and looped at top; period after signature; dashes used in place of, or to supplement periods.
4. Home-loving.	4. Forward slanting, rounded writing, conventionally formed.
5. Distrusts her sex.	5. Finals used to fill otherwise blank spaces; small, crowded writing with descending lines.
6. Maternal instinct.	6. Forward slanting writing; finals curling over to left.
7. Desires when aroused.	7. Forward slope, rounded hand, average pressure.
8. Spiritual-minded.	8. Downstrokes light; no shading; plain capitals.
9. Modest and satisfied.	9. Flourishes absent; plain capitals; inartistic writing.
10. Not strongly jealous.	10. Forward slanting, rounded writing, in medium or large hand.

Ideas and ideals should agree

Marriage is a mutual enterprise which means that the family group goes through life with co-pilots, and no marriage is truly a marriage without children. Children can always be adopted to round out the marriage relationship.

Religious ideals should be similar, moral ideals should be the same, and standards and patterns of social as well as personal conduct should parallel. If ideals are too different, one of the partners will begin to start making over the other person to his personality pattern. Infringement of personal freedom prevents the easy intimacy which is the relaxing and peaceful element in a happy marriage.

Whatever two people do individually, after they are married, if neither considers the action unusual or unfair, they can never seriously disagree on anything and can always be friends. But if there is a wide gap in their ideals or philosophies of life, then much of their married life will be spent in adjusting to each other's differences. Adjustment is not too difficult for short periods of time or for special occasions, but when it becomes necessary every day it becomes unendurable pain. You can prevent this anguish by finding out ahead of time what your proposed partner for life will be like.

What do you want in a husband or wife?

Whatever you may personally desire in a marriage partner you certainly will want your mate to have a likeable set of attitudes and talents. You will also want to weed out from consideration any individual who definitely has a bad slant on life or who has an unpleasant personality.

Turn back to Chapter Three and look over the groups of likeable personality qualities and the distasteful personality traits with the related indications in handwriting that you will find listed there. See how your marriageable friends stack up when you examine their handwriting, and, of course, how you yourself compare in likeable characteristics.

Why some marriages fail

1. Because the man marries purely for sexual satisfaction, there being little or no spiritual love for his wife.

A person of this type will write a coarse, muddy, heavy pressured hand.

Thomas E.

2. Because both partners are too selfish to make possible the give and take so necessary to keep a marriage from going on the rocks.

A person of this type will write a large, spread-out hand, with all the terminal strokes clipped short or absent.

Send me your
The following

3. Because one of the partners sees only the romantic side of marriage and expects the other to be ideal.

A person of this type will make frequent use of the underscore and of quotation, interrogation, and exclamation marks. Also, there will be a predominance of long loops. Letters will be disconnected and the style of writing will be original.

this summer
that our grand

4. Because one of the partners has an immature attitude toward life resulting in a feeling of confusion when the necessity comes for adjustment to the responsibilities of marriage.

An immature attitude toward life evidences itself in writing which is slightly larger than medium, rounded, with long final strokes, and with small letters made of varying sizes.

much for your

For Females Only

Find out whether you are the *career* type of woman or the *home-loving* type.

The career type woman

This type of woman is interested mainly in getting a job so that she may be independent financially. She wants to make a mark for herself in the world of careers. She is apt to be over-practical in matters of the heart and affections. There is a tendency to be adventurous in the field of morals.

Signs in handwriting

Long loop letters; disconnected letters; vertical, angular writing, in small hand; original style of writing.

bring to class
Shortened the

The home-loving type woman

This type of woman wants a husband, a home, and children. She thinks of marriage as her "career." She would be devoted, dependent, and self-sacrificing in her married life. She would put her home first, always. She would never let outside activities interfere with having her husband's supper ready on time, or with getting all the housework done.

Forward writing, in large or medium hand; full lower loops; letters all the same size; simple, unoriginal writing.

my daughter any and all

Ways to make a marriage a success

The love which brings two people together in marriage can turn to hate if it is not nurtured by both parties. The unselfish devotion of one person may keep a marriage from breaking up, but it takes two persons who are kind and considerate in their marital relationships to make the love of the wedding day last a lifetime.

Do not expect to be the same individual after you are married as you were before you were mated. Just be sure to modify your personality so that it reflects the good influence of your partner rather than the bad. Then there can be no complaint from either side of the marriage adventure.

If you keep a handwriting diary of your married life, or some kind of written running record so that you can study changes in your character as they are revealed in changes in your writing, you will know exactly what is happening to your personality. It will be up to you to call a halt and start off on new tangents of activity as the occasion necessitates.

Handwriting knowledge will make it possible for you to know the emotional make-up of your partner and fit in with it without friction or lack of understanding. This you should do, even at the expense of your own emotional happiness. Someone in the marriage pact has to assume the leadership and direction in riding out emotional storms.

The mutual enjoyment of common interests and common pleasures is another sure-fire way to make your marriage a success, and this grows out of being compatible in the first place. Areas of agreement are easier to arrive at, thus reducing the chances of unhappy arguments. Remember, as your wedding anniversaries become more numerous, think twice before you get twin beds!

10. Difficult people—how they write and how to handle them

Introducing "difficult people"

There are many types of *difficult* people, but there is one common denominator for all of them: they are *different* as well as difficult. That is, they have been difficult so long that they have affected their personalities strongly enough to change what started as a casual lapse into something habitual. When you meet difficult people in person they do not always reveal their character deficiency by mannerisms or by the way they talk. Often they try to hide their real character because they know you will not be pleased with them if you know the truth. However, they cannot hide it when they write something. Because they are different as well as difficult, they show the way they really are by the way they write.

When you observe handwriting which is *different* you can be sure the person who penned it is different, and he might also be difficult. The average person is not difficult. His handwriting will be similar to the average personality he possesses. That is, he will mirror in his script only a small amount of irritating or unpleasant characteristics. Being difficult occasionally is quite different from being hard to handle all the time.

Negative people

When you come across a person who obstructs easy living by assuming a negative attitude to anything that is presented you have a hard personality problem to solve. If you are one of these people yourself you are in a doubly difficult situation.

Negative individuals write smaller than normal, have a vertical or backward angle to their writing, cross their t's with a firm, short stroke, low-down on the t-stem, execute capitals with little or no embellishment, pen their script with slow speed, and may or may not have hooks and heavy downstrokes in their writing, depending on the degree of negativism in their writing.

In dealing with these people you seldom present them with a "Yes or No," proposition thus preventing them from taking one side or the other. Also, you never let them know that you have definite opinions on anything; always attribute strong statements of viewpoints to other people. They cannot, then, turn their negativism on you personally. If you find it necessary to make them like you, try to give them plenty of opportunity to talk and express themselves. After they enjoy being negative, they generally will switch to a positive attitude. Their turnabout way of thinking is only their initial way of reacting to life rather than their continuous pattern of behavior.

out some details

opportunities offered

Would you please

Fanatics

Of all the types of personality pests the fanatic seems the worst. He has proceeded so far to the extreme in his personality decline that most persons immediately think of "last-ditch defenses" to ward off the irritations and emotional upsets possible when the fanatic makes his appearance.

The fanatic may be defined as an individual who is so sold on a *single idea* that he feels a compulsion to make everything else in the world conform to his understanding of that narrow thought. He may be a religious zealot, a rabid reformer, an insistent militarist, or he may turn his overconcern into negative channels by thinking of ways to thwart the activities of ordinary people whom he imagines are trying to interfere with the expansion of his pet project.

Fanatics are only dangerous when they become confused. Most leaders become mildly fanatic when they see the need for drawing attention to their particular Cause. We expect those who have faith in their work to back it up with strong statements and precipitous action. But we become alarmed when leadership takes a fanatical turn and extreme action is urged. We are rightly anxious since we realize that any off-balancing of human activity is dangerous for society in general. Fanatics in a state of mental confusion are apt to upset their environment when they become too insistent that others believe as they do.

You can tell the dangerous fanatic by writing which is extremely heavy-pressured, letter forms which are narrow and compressed and with the lower loops of one line entangled with the upper loops of the line beneath it.

In dealing with a fanatic you must be definite and determined, explaining that, at this particular time, you are not interested in what he has to offer or what he wants to talk about. He will understand firmness since he is imbued with it himself. If you show any signs of weakness, he will interpret courteous consideration and tact as a sign of indecision and will strain to convert you to his way of thinking. You will not be able to get rid of this person's company. If you manage to be out of your office, he will pester you on the telephone.

Actually, no matter how you begin your relations with a fanatic you will always end up the same, getting emotional and deciding on drastic action. By asserting your point of view in the beginning, before you let your feelings build up to an unpleasant climax, you can handle the fanatic with a minimum of personal discomfort.

Suspicious persons

Suspicious people, destructive as they are to themselves, are even more detrimental when they are part of a group, whether it be a church choir or a downtown office. In a factory they could actually slow up production by their depressing attitude. A suspicious individual immediately thinks of something wrong when a new plan or procedure is offered. He takes more time to do ordinary things because he must first check to eliminate his fear of mistakes that other people are always making. He undermines the self-confidence that other workers may have; he generates distrust and contributes to uneasiness and unhappiness.

How does a suspicious person write? He will write small, his a's and o's will be closed at the top, he will turn back his ending strokes, his script will be vertical or backhand, and he will tend to keep his writing as simplified as possible. Extremely suspicious people will slur their letter forms and dot their i's close to the top of the i.

The best way to deal with suspicious people is to act natural and unaffected. Any attempt to gain their confidence only makes them more suspecting. That is the essence of getting along with them.

If you have the problem of preventing suspicious people from making trouble in your organization, you should show a special interest in these people, indirectly through your Personnel Manager, to find out and eliminate real causes for distrust, such as promises made and not kept. Your next step is to examine their suitability for the jobs they are doing with the object of reassigning them to other places in your organization. Whatever you do to contribute to their happiness, through a chance for fuller creative expression or by an opportunity for a more logical use of their talents, will also result in a decrease in their suspiciousness and an increase in the general pleasantness of the group.

Suspicious people have had bad breaks and an extra amount of worrisome experiences which have filled them with unhappiness and feelings of pessimism. They may be highly-talented, loyal, and cooperative if the reason for their distrustful thinking is understood.

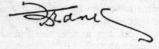

Argumentative people

People who enjoy arguing are unpleasant to deal with since they are also opinionated. They are not afraid to discuss any issue whatever because they know in advance that whatever you present as an argument will be worthless in the light of what they know about the subject.

The handwriting of the argumentative person will be full of hooks, heavy in pressure, forward-slanting, and will have many ending strokes that point downward and to the right like drawn daggers.

There are many ways to deal with the arguer, depending

upon who he is. If he is a friend whom you must have around, perhaps a business associate, you would do best to agree with him whenever you can without compromising your own personal standards. You can gain his confidence more by refusing to argue than by giving in when you know it will only lead to an emotional disagreement. If he is a casual acquaintance you can simply change the subject to something that he will have a mild opinion on, allow him to express it, and then get on with the important business of the moment. He will never listen to you seriously until he has had a chance to demonstrate his argumentative superiority. Arguing is a form of verbal aggression, common with many men and with women who have masculine tendencies.

Came at Amherst

Narrow-minded people

Narrow-minded people lack imagination and hence are unable to see life beyond the end of their noses. They are very difficult to deal with because they can be advanced in their thinking only a few ideas beyond what they know. Their writing will be narrow, that is, the letters will be drawn close to each other.

People of this sort have to be agreed with in order to get along with them. You cannot change their minds by arguing with them. Your only recourse is to introduce a few new ideas every time you talk to them, but never appearing dogmatic or demanding in your attitude. After a long time they will believe you and will become a bit more open-minded in your presence. But that is as far as you will ever get in advancing them in their mental fixations.

Arthur

Summary

There are many more "difficult" people in the world than just the negative person, the fanatic, the suspicious person, argumentative individuals, and those with narrow minds. The important point to keep in mind is that these troublesome humans show their traits in their script, penning hands just as "different" as they are "different."

After a little practice you will be able to pick out quickly the hard-to-get-along-with people and deal with them to your own satisfaction. Graphology is that easy—and that useful!

11. Using handwriting to achieve better health

In looking for health symptoms in handwriting it must be assumed that the writing under study is not the product of a person who has had any kind of nerve, muscle, or brain injury that would affect the mechanisms controlling the hand movements. This would disturb the rhythm and free movement of muscles, definitely interfering with individual expression. The lack of muscular coordination would paint a false picture of the personality.

The following specimen of writing was penned by a person afflicted with spastic paralysis. Notice the halted rhythm in the script since each letter had to be formed separately.

inhabitants

Handwriting and your health

Your state of health will affect especially the pressure and the rhythm of your handwriting. If you are in good health your writing will be smooth and rhythmic with continuously formed strokes. If you are in poor health there will be a major variation or change in the pressure and rhythm features of your handwriting. Because the writing movement is linked to the nervous system, any physical or mental change or disorder will be reflected in the writing produced.

dish of ice cream

took with it

Poor health.

Good health.

Heart trouble

If you have an irregular heart beat this will cause a distinct tremor as you write and your pen will record it in the form of a notch in the upper loop strokes of the l and h.

This sensitivity is somewhat similar to the delicacy of the lie-detector mechanism, except that there is no power source to magnify the impulse for charting. Hence, the fact that the heart beat disturbance is recorded as a break in the rhythm of the stroke just before it makes the descent is easy evidence of the registering of this heart tremor.

Breathing disorders

When a person has trouble breathing, due to some lung disorder or other interference, there may be rifts or slight catches in the loops and curves above the line, if the ailment is serious enough to reflect the disturbances in habitual breathing rhythm.

Nearsightedness

Nearsighted people will always begin a new line of writing so that it slants at a different angle from the one preceding it. In addition, the line of writing will be uneven.

Nervousness

Tremulous strokes reveal nervousness and when accompanied by final strokes descending to the right, tell of a timid and mildly fearful nature.

Because a nervous person reacts immediately to unpleasantness in his environment, he is susceptible to asthma, allergies, or ulcers, depending upon how his personality is put together. The nervous person is also an easy victim of psychosomatic diseases. When a person has a complete nervous breakdown he has very little control over his handwriting and it will be considerably disorganized from its conventional arrangement. That is why, if you keep watching your handwriting, you will be able to observe when you are getting "off the beam" and you can then take steps to work yourself back to a clear course.

Arthritis

If arthritis strikes, your hands will eventually be affected and your writing will change. Your writing will be shaky, light-pressured, and irregular. It will never be delicate in style and will tend toward awkwardness in construction.

A state of depression

When lines of writing are very descending you can be sure that the person who has penned the writing is suffering from some form of sadness. It may be despondency or it may be cold grief. His spirits, experiencing a psychic lag, cause his script to be written below the normal line of writing.

If you are the depressed one in this case, and your *words* as well as lines descend, then you should do something definite to lift yourself from your downhearted moodiness. A state of depression can become habitual and is never helpful. Realize that you can rise above misfortune just as easily as becoming dragged down by it. Force yourself to write on a straight base line or actually slant your writing upward. This simple handwriting therapy will help you to concentrate on constructive optimism and you will soon rid yourself of the "blues."

This summer

very much —

would cost

Heart trouble starting.

is made up

rich soiled land

Breathing difficulty.

though that the
a living. you
effective only be
industry and o
Contribute yours

Nearsightedness.

The weather has
turned warm,
all people are
differant,

Written a few weeks after a severe heart attack.

whole auditorium

Nervousness combined with timidity.

The effect of cold upon handwriting.

Handwriting written in a cold room will be different than
script penned in a place where the writer suffers no physical

discomforts. Cold numbs the hand and definitely disturbs the natural, rhythmic movement of a healthy, free-flowing handwriting.

Study your energy output

The degree of pressure you exert on your writing will tell you about your energy output and its relationship to your health. If you write with an extremely heavy pressure you are wasting some of your vitality since life is not meant to be lived at high tension at all moments.

If you pen your script with a very light pressure you will be healthy and mentally serene, provided there are no strange formations in your handwriting, but you will also lack the will-power and drive to get you over or out of emergency physical dangers. Therefore, it would be to your benefit to exert yourself more if you are a light-pressured and an energy-deficient writer.

If your writing is average-pressured you will be able to do what most people around you do. However, this merely places you in the "average" category which means you have a "run-of-the-mill" state of health.

For successful achievement it is necessary to be able to increase one's energy output at strategic times, and this is not possible for those who are under-active consistently or for those who live life on an even plane. So the sad conclusion is this: Aggressive, forceful living is conducive to success, at least materially, but it also undermines one's health by burning up energy too fast and too often.

Excessively energetic people can improve their health by controlling their vitality so that it is channeled only into constructive pursuits, preferably in areas of minimum emotional stress. Frequent vacations or physical respites would also conserve the energy drain.

Heavy Pressure.

Medium Pressure.

I would like to

Light Pressure.

What about fear?

Fear and health are closely related. This is because there is a strong emotional reaction when a situation is frightening enough. Assume a lion breaks loose from a cage in a zoo at which you happen to be a visitor. Unless you are a very extraordinary person you will experience the feeling of fear when you see the lion rushing toward you. You will tremble, become pale, your muscles will contract, and you will either run for your life or stand frozen in your tracks, too paralyzed to move. You might possibly faint. These are all fear reactions.

If the lion reaches you and is about to attack you, a scream will be your next fear response. If, however, you find it possible to take flight, your body will be prepared to keep you moving at a faster rate than you usually run, and without getting tired as easily. Stimulated by the emotion of fear, sugar will be secreted into your blood in large quantities so as to give you added strength and endurance to make your flight. Your pulse will beat more quickly so as to accelerate the circulation of the blood, and digestive processes will be stopped so that all the blood may be used to help get you out of danger. In other words, it is clearly apparent that when you are terribly frightened your body expects you to do something about it. Some action must be taken.

Primitive man acted physically under the fear impetus and ran away. Civilized man stayed his ground, sometimes fighting back and in other cases "swallowing" his fears. How you react to fear will determine the state of your mental and your physical health. It is easy to see that undue emotional stress, induced by fear, will upset the nervous system and change the nature of handwriting.

When fear rules

If fear becomes a habitual reaction in your life you will become "touchy," sensitive, and "on edge." Instead of your emotions (fear-dominated) being in the background where they are helpful in giving meaning to life, they act as a screen between you and your environment. It is as if the screen were charged with electricity and every time anything touches it you respond with a current of emotional excitation, because you are frightened. The cause of this ever-present feeling of fear is a chronic condition of nervousness, the result of your body's need continually to relieve you of your built-up tenseness so that you do not have a nervous breakdown.

If your nervousness is due to fear you will write with a light or variable pressure, your base line of writing will be wavy or irregular and there will be lance-like t-crossings (heavy at the beginning of the stroke and shading off to a point) in your script.

This is the kind of fearsomeness that can be controlled, changed, and minimized as far as its harmful effects are concerned since it is not destructive as long as the individual is able to recognize it for what it is. When fear is faced it does not disappear but it ceases completely to rule the emotions. Thus the individual has a good chance to get back to normal, happy living.

What you should know about fear

Since fear is transient, do not let it affect you permanently. The mental hospitals are full of people who started out with what was once only a mild mental disorder but which somehow developed into a serious derangement. Fear had become a habit so that when undue stress came the nerve-patterns were ready and waiting, so to speak, to carry the message.

Do not project your fears into the future. Give yourself the benefit of the doubt, remembering that, according to the law of averages, there are just as many chances in your favor as there are against you.

Fear is very apt to start a chain reaction, one fear suggesting another, or recalling old fears. For that reason you should eliminate fear from your thinking, except of course, reasonable anxieties, such as fear of real danger.

Self-confidence, proper food, clothing, and shelter, financial security, successful achievement, laughing at life, trying to understand other people, a common-sense opinion of one's self, and faith in some religion, will all assist in eliminating fear from our lives.

Mild fear is normal; strong fear is not.

Summary

Since your handwriting is a pen picture of your mind and body in action, it reveals the true state of your thought processes and your body tone. That is why your writing reveals how healthy you are.

You should especially watch your pressure and your rhythm since these are quickly affected by poor health.

Overstimulation may be exciting you to an unhealthy energy drain. It may also be wearing upon a particular part of your physique, such as your heart.

The facts on fear must be faced. You are living in an age which is anything but free from fear; courage must be cultivated.

The special phases of mental health are not discussed in this chapter but may be studied in Chapter 12: "Alerting Yourself To Danger Symptoms Through Handwriting."

Finally, keep this "Handwriting Health Chart" to guide you along the paths to better health.

My Handwriting Health Chart

.... Month ... Day ... Year ...... Simple Statement of Fact

....

....

....

....

....

....

....

....

Using this chart

Every few months jot down the date and pen a simple statement of fact on the same line, such as: "I just returned from a trip to New York."

Compare your writing on the different dates and you will be able to plot the progress of your health, mental and physical. Your handwriting will reveal the essential changes.

Dangers to watch for:

1. Erratic and uneven pressure indicates mental strain.

2. Illegible script denotes a dissatisfaction with reality and a strong desire to experiment to escape the boredom of frustration.

3. Muddy writing denotes sensuousness. If your writing suddenly degenerates to this you are easily susceptible to strong stimulants.

4. Extreme light-pressured writing reveals a desire to be relieved of responsibilities.

5. Sudden flourishes suggest a tendency to exaggerate which means that you are losing your good judgment.

6. Extreme angularity, hooks, lance-like t-crossings, and other negative signs in writing denote that you are getting "cranky" and belligerent. Get back to your old self and remain constructive.

12. Alerting yourself to danger symptoms through handwriting

Your handwriting is the outward expression of inner tensions, disturbances, or other changes that may be happening to you, so subtly, perhaps, and so gradually, that you might easily not be consciously aware of them. Before you, therefore, is a mirror of yourself. It is a pen picture. It is a testament in script of the way you are at the particular moment that you write and it is an accurate forecast of the direction in which you are going.

It is in your writing that you can observe, and profit by, the danger signals warning you of possible blocks to healthy and happy living. Some of these warning signs may simply say, "Slow Down"; others may advise you to come to a dead stop; still others may caution you to change direction. Your script should be examined for indications of disaster that could happen to you. Remember, it has to get cloudy before it can rain.

Watch for a change in your way of writing

What are some of the danger signals in handwriting? The first thing to beware of is a definite change from your usual way of writing. If you generally write a clear, detailed hand and shift to a careless, diffuse form of writing in which the letters are difficult to identify, then you may be on your way to a nervous breakdown. What has happened is that you have begun to lose your sense of purpose and security, and you have allowed yourself to jump from one thing to another as you go about seeking some way to get back on your feet. Troubles of one kind or another have jolted you from your

179

normal routine, and fear of the unpredictable future has "unnerved" you, so to speak. This is reflected in your handwriting, which, as mentioned, is the motor expression of your loosened-up nervous system. When you have a complete nervous breakdown you will be unable to write legibly at all.

Signs of mental illness

Everyone has the possibility of becoming mentally ill since it is the next step away from a state of sanity. Therefore, we could all profit from a close look at our handwriting to see if we are leaning in that direction.

If you are on the erratic and unreal road to loss of reason you will show it in a number of ways, depending upon the nature of your mental derangement.

If your personality is in the process of splitting into two parts so that one half of you is fast losing contact with the actual world about you, there will be odd letter styles, queer arrangements of words, and a tendency to make involved flourishes. Words will be repeated and underlined. Lower and upper loops will be exaggerated and will be entangled with each other. Pressure will tend to be heavy.

If the mind has experienced complete flight from reality, the handwriting will be impossible to read since it will mirror subconscious thoughts rather than registering the known world of consciousness.

If the mind is conscious of its environment but confused and restless, the writing may run in all directions without regard to base lines, and will cross and re-cross like the tracks in a railroad yard terminal. Mental disturbance means manual disturbance.

For the average person the prospect of mental illness is quite far off. However, when the average individual becomes mentally sick, he indicates progress in this direction by an increasing illegibility of his script, if it was at first clear and easy to read. When the illegibility is complete, and the numerous other supporting signs of mental illness are present, then the person is completely ill. *How* ill he is becomes a matter for medical study and consideration. The worth of psychographology is in detecting sickness of the mind before it becomes an unpleasant *unreality!*

The person who penned the following specimen is a patient in a mental institution (Buffalo State Hospital), suffering from psychoneurosis, often referred to as "nervous breakdown."

For the moment of writing, at least, this person was able

to effect enough muscular-mental organization to put down the dictated words in very legible form. The light pressure, the extreme variation in the letter forms, and the crippled drawing of the letter "s" in the second "This" are the tell-tale signs of mental confusion and nerve strain.

This is a beautiful
This is what I thin
you.

"Manic Phase of Manic Depressive Psychosis," is the official diagnosis of the writer of the following specimen, a patient at Buffalo State Hospital. The disorganization of his personality is plainly pictured, not only in his letter forms but in his odd and confused spelling. Note the extreme weakness of his t-crossings, and the lack of most of the i-dots.

Ths a Beautif
n weon at a Buti
day
this is what i th
off you

Recognizing schizophrenia

Schizophrenia, or the "split personality," which is the most widespread of the serious mental ills, is easy to recognize in its advanced stages but is most dangerous in that it does not reveal itself easily in handwriting in its early development. That is, if one checked his handwriting only sporadically he would not see the insidious progress of this disease. A regularly recorded handwriting diary, making it possible to observe script for signs of change or shift into involved letter-forms or into thread-like illegibility, indicating flight from reality, would make it possible to check schizophrenia by early hospitalization.

According to Dr. George S. Stevenson, New York medical consultant to the National Association for Mental Health, victims of schizophrenia now have at least a 60 per cent chance of partial or complete recovery if they get early and adequate hospital treatment.

Schizophrenic Psychosis of the Catatonic Type.
(*Official Diagnosis: Buffalo State Hospital, N.Y.*)

Lucidity and legibility in mental illness

In certain kinds of mental illnesses there are times when the "patients" seem to be normal because they present logical arrangements of ideas. If you happen upon them when they are in these brief moments of lucidity and you ask them to write something for you, you will be surprised when you look at their script. It will be legible, or nearly so. Since handwriting must mirror the mood of the moment of writing, it must reflect the flash of sanity that has brightened the otherwise sick mind.

If you look carefully at the specimens illustrated below you will notice a few mirrors from the subconscious, along with the conscious reflections. Note the small s's with the double-backed strokes, the peculiar formation in the middle of the w in "what," and the odd capital I. (Paranoid Psychosis).

A person unfamiliar with the handwriting of the paranoiac would judge this specimen, because of its extreme legibility, to be perfectly normal.

This is a beautiful day.

This is what I think of you.

The quick, brown fox jumps

The quick brown

The quick brown fox

Paranoid Psychosis.
(Official Diagnosis: Buffalo State Hospital, N.Y.)

Notice the odd-shaped letter forms in these paranoid specimens: the q in the "quick" in the second example, the q in the "quick" in the fourth, and the f in "fox" in the fourth.

Mild mental illness may be serious

It is obvious that when a mild mental disorder develops into a situation that requires the hospitalization of the person, this is serious for all concerned. But there is one type of mental aberration which is more dangerous in its mild stage than when it becomes severe. This is the victim of melancholia.

Do you recall the last suicide that happened in your local community? Was it not someone that people least expected? Of course, close relatives knew that he was feeling "depressed," but they gave the typical layman's diagnosis: "It couldn't be too serious or he'd be sick in bed." For some reason or other, nonmedical-minded individuals seem to think that as long as you can walk around there can be nothing really wrong with you.

But a person who suffers a "fit of depression" is as sick as if he had just severed his jugular vein. During his melancholia he may take his life.

You can pick out the person who is meandering down the sorry path of melancholia by looking for one of the simplest signs in handwriting diagnosis: the drooping or pointing down of the last word or words in many of the lines of writing.

Melancholia associated with Involutional Period.
(Official Diagnosis: Buffalo State Hospital, N.Y.)

Are you becoming a neurotic?

Because the neurotic is so completely maladjusted to life he mirrors himself rather fully in the way he writes. If you are in danger of becoming a serious neurotic, with all the conflicts and tensions inherent in a strong neurosis, you will reveal your lack of psychic stability in your script.

Your handwriting will vary in the angle of inclination; that is, some of your words will slant forward, some backward, and some will be formed vertically. There will be variations in pressure, assorted t-crossings, varying i-dots, awkward letter shapes, flourished capitals, loop letters of all sizes, and sudden shifts from legible to diffuse writing. Spacing will be of poor proportion and rhythm will be lacking.

The neurotic person is also an escapist seeking to avoid reality by refusing to be pinned down to any definite set of actions. If you are on the way to becoming a neurotic don't worry about it if you are very wealthy or if you are a genius —which you could be—since neither very rich people nor geniuses have to be concerned with their personality make-up! Or so it seems.

Two neurotics.

Escape through introspection.

Escape through physical activity.

The criminal is in some cases a mentally unbalanced person who will not accept the world of the good citizen as his world. He prefers an "underworld" of his own where he can hide his identity, thereby escaping the responsibility of having to face up to the harsh realities of everyday living. To murder, to steal, or to assault are the criminal's subconscious attempts to destroy or upset the world he does not want to exist. His handwriting will be abnormal to fit his character.

From abnormality the script will degenerate to indicate mental illness. From mild derangement it will, if given time, change to indicate derangement with intent to destroy— "criminal insanity."

Temporary mental flight

The illustration below is a good example of how a disturbed state of mind affects a person's writing. It is the script of a young man a few hours before he was married. He frankly admitted he was flustered, and his script is perfect proof of his mental confusion.

Interruptions may signal illness

The way you breathe and the way you write are strongly connected. Any interruption in the rhythm of breathing will be noticed in a similar halt or break in portions of the writing movement. This is especially reflected in the upper loops of small letters since this detail of letter formation involves a change in direction in the writing movement and it is here that a person with a heart ailment, for instance, will reveal his weakness. There will be a slight catch or indentation in the top part of the loop of a small h or l just before the pen begins to make the return trip to complete the lower portion of the letter.

Heart strain should be avoided if hitches of this nature are discovered in your handwriting. The heavier and the more frequent the appearance of catches or other interruptions in handwriting, the more serious the ailment can be.

Signs of internal disorder

Muddiness or heavy, scrawly writing is an indication of some kind of internal disorder. The whole bodily system is involved in some kind of maladjustment when handwriting is heavy-pressured and crudely executed. Often there are obsessions in the personality or over-concernments in the mind which could result in disorders often referred to as "emotionally induced illnesses." Chemical secretions from overactive glands will affect the smooth-functioning of the nervous system and will register in the undue stresses and strains in the handwriting.

When muddiness in writing is combined with a marked slowing down of the writing speed there is grave danger that the writer will develop obsessions, phobias, or other mental tangents that could move him quickly down the road toward a serious mental disorder.

Frustration evidenced in handwriting

The appearance of hooks, tightly-knotted a's and o's, and the pulling backward of the ending strokes of the last letter in words are all sure signs of extreme frustration which may lead to acts of sudden impulse apt to destroy the peace and decorum of your daily life. Frustrated people build up a background of resentment, negativism, dislike, disapproval, and, in some cases, despair, which makes them quickly susceptible to participation or initiation of sudden changes, whether for their own good or not.

Frustrated people are "ready" to argue, they are prepared to fight, they enjoy gossip, they seek to resist and they seek to upset the "status quo" of a situation to achieve a taste of excitement.

Emotional problems are costly

Emotional problems, if not solved, can cost money. According to Dr. Harry Levinson, director of the Division of Industrial Mental Health at the Menninger Foundation, Topeka, Kansas, emotional problems are annually costing industry many millions of dollars.

"About half of industrial absences," he stated at a University of Buffalo industrial relations conference, "are due to emotional causes. There are about 15,000 industrial deaths a year and about 2,000,000 disabling accidents, 80-90 per cent of which are caused by psychological failures. One out of 50 workers is a problem drinker."

Dr. Levinson further remarked that emotional problems were not limited to workers and pointed out that executives were plagued with feelings of inadequacy in the work expected of them.

If this is true, as it certainly seems to be, then it would do well for us to use our handwriting as a guide to understand what is happening to us emotionally, with the purpose in mind of doing something about danger symptoms we might see in our script.

Is old age creeping up on you?

Your handwriting will tell you whether or not you are aging. If you still have the physical strength of your youth, your script will be firm-pressured, without too much variation or change within the body of the writing. But if age is beginning to slow you down and weaken your physical stamina, your writing will be weakly-written and will waver. The older you are, the shakier your handwriting will become.

Illness very often causes writing to lack pressure and to appear as if written on a moving train because of the wavy base line and the slowly-formed letters. Disease is Nature's way of aging human beings, hence we would expect the writing of a sick person to look like that of a person who was aging.

If your handwriting indicates aging when it should show

the full-blooded vigor of youth it would be wise to have a complete physical and mental check-up.

This is the handwriting of a 90-year-old man, still in full possession of his mental faculties, but showing some of the signs of physical aging.

In contrast, note the above script, officially diagnosed as: "Organic Psychosis due to Senile Changes." (Buffalo State Hospital, N.Y.)

Are you afraid of drugs or alcohol?

Fear of becoming an alcoholic or of succumbing to drug addiction is present in the minds of many people. Any habitual activity along these lines will, of course, reflect itself in the way you write since the damage to your health will show in the deterioration of your script. But, if you have the type of personality that will be more than normally attracted to alcoholic use because of your character pattern, this fact will be clearly indicated in the way you write.

Thick, muddy writing with heavy shading will warn you that you have the psychic make-up that may seek abnormal physical satisfaction of one sort or another. Your sensuous nature may call for alcohol, drugs, or perhaps for large amounts of food to satisfy your physical cravings.

Prolonged use of either drugs or alcohol will evidence itself in a definite interference with the natural rhythm of a handwriting. The dulling effect of alcohol upon the mind will obviously slow down and confuse the writing movement resulting in a script characterized by awkwardness in style, cramped letter formations, and jagged punctuation marks. The distortion of the mind and the lack of muscular coordination will mirror a handwriting equally tangled and hesitant.

Anyone can become an alcoholic—and these people may mirror you

There are many other reasons why you might be attracted to alcohol; the blight of a sensuous nature is only one reason and applies especially to a particular type of person. The other reasons cut across the whole fabric of life and touch every social class and each economic level. We are obviously living in an age in which it is practically impossible for anyone to escape from the advertising of alcohol or from its easy access, in public and in private. Since our society is now plagued with the presence of some four million problem drinkers, with the number growing as our population increases, it would be extremely helpful if you could know in advance if you had any special propensities in your personality that would advance you into alcoholism quicker than the average person.

Most medical authorities agree that drinking in the emotionally immature person is more dangerous than in the well-adjusted individual. Another way of saying this is to state that the "weak" personality would succumb to alcoholic distresses more promptly than would a "strong" personality. Weakness, in this case, refers to instability, a feeling of insecurity, or a general inability to keep in rhythmic and happy coordination with your environment. Hence, if you are "at odds" with life and do not have the personality structure to handle day-to-day difficulties so that you are satisfied, then you have two strikes against you when you taste alcohol. Addiction to alcohol is the final unpleasant step.

Three hypersensitive men under treatment for alcoholism

Go to your
dealer to-day.
Pick up official
rules and Entry!

Now is the time for all good men come to the aid their party. By: looks of Partew I am sure it is. Democratic Party should aid.

Like ranks of herald angels, a display

Although the writing specimens above may look like feminine script, they belong to three men who happen to have more than the normal amount of female characteristics and hence write a "female" hand. Absolute sex is one of the facts that the handwriting analyst cannot state for certain; he can only point out the relative possession of male as against female characteristics.

If you will compare the three specimens with each other you will notice the following similarities: easy legibility, fast writing, over-inflated loops, increase of pressure or hooks at the ends of words, and a rhythmic sweep to the forward-slanting script. These are all indications of personalities that are easily carried away by any excesses.

Control of the writing movement is beginning to deteriorate as indicated in specimens (2) and (3), where certain strokes are elongated without reason (the D in Democratic, for example). The loops of one line are entangled with the loops of another.

In specimen (1) the compulsion to drink has so affected this person that he reveals his attempt to hold back the natural impulsiveness of his nature by writing that is unnaturally contracted. Rigidity is replacing free and easy action but it is causing tension of another type than his original tension which helped make him an alcoholic.

If you write like the above people you would do well to keep clear of alcohol.

In the illustration below, the mental imbalance is shown by poor word and line spacing, the extreme variation in the size of the various small letters, and the vindictive surges of pressure in the strokes and the t-crossings. Resentment has replaced what would otherwise be a cooperative personality. Subconsciously he is irritated by his alcoholic addiction.

Slow and serious alcoholics under treatment

As previously mentioned, alcohol has an appeal for those persons who can employ it to lift them out of a dull routine or away from an over-serious philosophy of life. The illustrations below fall in this classification, since they are all hand-writings of what we would call, "average, sober-minded citizens." Alcoholism, however, has hit each one and resulted in a certain degree of personality and physiological disturbance.

Thank you america

Muscular coordination is extremely poor in the above specimen. Note the total lack of rhythm in the word, "America."

John and Norma Merrill realize even happiness has 'its' responsibilities. They wouldn't change their life for anything.

Nervous system damage is indicated in the extreme variations in pressure in the sample above. Mental confusion is shown by the corrective writing or "mending" in the three words, "happiness," "life," and "anything."

What's it like to live in

Puerto Rico today?

"The climate is probably as

close to Paradise as any man

will ever see"

Mental deterioration is shown in the above writing in an inability to maintain an even slant, the tremor in the e in "Puerto," and in the squarish R in "Rico." Note, too, the shape of some of the odd o and a formations.

This book is an attempt to record the present and to offer some illumination for the future.

This specimen is awkward and uncoordinated, ranging from excessive contraction to loosely-controlled writing strokes.

These agencies as well, had did this Commission with their sup in bringing about the public accep of the law.

The instability of this individual is evidenced by all the signs of personality insecurity, from changes in pressure and letter size to lack of reasonable embellishment in the capital letters and a regression to backhand writing.

Experiments at The Handwriting Institute, Inc., of New York City, using a Graphodyne Stylus (equipped with a strain gauge) to measure and record script variation in persons under the influence of alcohol, clearly indicated that a raggedness of stroke and a definite disturbance in rhythm (due to impairment of muscular and neural control) results as the brain becomes befogged with alcohol.

Courtesy of
The Handwriting Institute, Inc.

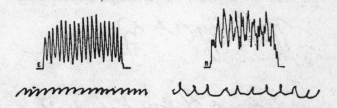

| (Normal) | (Alcoholic) |

How alcohol "roughens" handwriting,
as recorded by Graphodyne measurement technique.

As alcohol is imbibed beyond the body's ability to "burn it up," it causes damage to one's physiognomy, in the beginning minor and finally major. Dr. Melvin H. Knisely, head of the Department of Anatomy at the Medical College of South Carolina, speaking at the 28th International Congress on Alcohol and Alcoholism (September 19, 1968), was of the opinion that even social drinking may result in a great deal of damage to the brain, noting that the killing of a few brain cells with each "happy" state of inebriation all adds up since the damage each time is permanent.

He related that oxygen starvation takes place during a heavy intake of alcohol because of changes in the blood and blood vessels; brain cells are destroyed when their oxygen supply is cut off. He reported that recent research has shown that alcohol induces thickening of the blood with resultant blockage of blood flow affecting some brain cells.

Because brain damage is cumulative, even if only as few as 10,000 of the brain's 10 to 18 billion cells were destroyed after each social drinking session, this could be significant over an extended period of time, with heavy drinking underlining the problem. Brain damage causes one to forget; it blurs whatever sense of order one possesses and it interferes with one's general efficiency. Dr. Knisely observed that the bodies of "Skid Row" drunks revealed such extensive destruction of cells that their brains were worthless for teaching use with medical students studying brain structure.

Here are some handwriting specimens of derelicts who have had severe brain damage due to heavy drinking. The ragged strokes, the extreme disturbance in normal writing rhythm and the aggressive digs of extra pressure are writing changes that can be observed in all these specimens, with differences due to the variations in the "resistance power" of each personality, physically and psychologically.

Oxygen starvation with pilots

In experiments with pilots flying at high altitudes (*Fortune Magazine*, Sept., 1940), when oxygen deficiency resulted the airmen experienced convulsions, mental aberrations and severe pains. If this condition of oxygen starvation had continued, brain damage would have been the next result.

Army laboratory experiments at Wright Field further discovered that reflexes were so slowed up by the decrease of needed oxygen to the brain that pilots, recording in script what was happening to them, soon found that their handwriting went out of control because of the interference with their muscular control—caused by the malfunctioning of parts of their brain mechanisms.

Here is the beginning of a pilot's written record, with the script appearing quite normal although somewhat "agitated":

Now the pilot loses all control as he becomes "oxygen starved":

Recognizing the drug addict

Because of its deteriorating effect upon the nervous system, the drug addict leaves a number of tell-tale traces in any writing that he executes. There will be the expected sudden spurts or surges of pressure causing the writing to look blotchy, and there will be various indications of lack of rhythmic muscular coordination. But every so often there will be a word in the writing which will be partly rewritten or containing tangled letters, as if the mind went out of control for the moment due to some reaction from the powerful narcotic.

In the following illustration, penned by a drug user who had been using narcotics for three years and written while he was under the weakening effects of the drugs, the word "three" is the giveaway word. It is the handwriting of a 21-year-old young man.

The specimens of handwriting below are those of a 25-year-old man who was a confirmed drug addict at the time he made these notes. His addiction is revealed in the confused u in "Vaughn," as well as the extra-heavy base-pressure in most of the letters.

Sweet + Gentle
G. Gibbs

Goober Peas
R. Draper

House of Blue Lights
Chuck Miller

The drug addiction of this 40-year-old woman is particularly indicated by the erratic formation of the n in the word "not."

I intend to voluntarily com
myself to the Buffalo City
not later than April 26,
I intend to forever disconti
use of narcotic drugs and.
that my voluntary comm.
for cure of mis-drug adde

Are you antagonistic toward other people?

You have a real weight to drag through life if your handwriting reveals that you are antagonistic toward other people. If there are hooks and catches of the pen in your writing then you are in real danger of annoying great numbers of people. The sad part about this situation is that you will never know just who the people are whom you bother because of your aggressive attitude. They won't take the time to tell you. After all, why should they? They just won't give you any business, invite you to their homes, or cater to you in any way. They will just leave you alone.

An antagonistic attitude toward the rest of the world is built up through successions of failures of one sort or another, or because of some soul-searing disappointment. Once you decide that it is you who are out of step and not the world you will discover that people will accept you for what you consider yourself to be. You place your own value on yourself, and that is the price tag that shows. Think well and happily of yourself, and you will find your associates thinking likewise.

Do successful salesmen frown?

Note the hooks and catches in these antagonistic people.

Lagging mental maturity—a real danger

One of the great social deficiencies that many adults suffer from, and do not realize, is the mature mental attitude that is supposed to go with adulthood. It might be stated as "lagging maturity." The attainment of maturity or "growing up" as it is often called, is a progressive, and sometimes painful process. A certain amount of experiences are necessary in order to "understand" life's real meanings. For one reason or another a good number of persons are halted in their progress toward this natural goal of all humans. They never grow up.

Large, schoolboyish writing, slowly written, indicates this, together with flourished capitals and shaded down-strokes.

As a person advances toward maturity his capital letters become less flourished (but not plain), his script is penned with increasing speed, and the writing tends to become much smaller. As the writing decreases in size, the capital letters also decrease in proportion. If the writing gets smaller and the capitals go the other way and become inordinately larger and billowy, then the individual is an insecure mixture of extreme maturity on the one hand and absolute childishness on the other.

employee world

I sure was sorry

New York and Pennsylv

Examples of lagging mental maturity.

Lee Harvey Oswald and Sirhan Sirhan . . . Assassins

Here is the handwriting of Lee Harvey Oswald, the assassin of President John F. Kennedy. Notice the muddiness of the script, the digs of aggressive pressure and the angular, cutlike strokes that indicate an individual who acts vindictively toward those whom he does not like. The slow-moving hand tells us also that this person would act obsessively rather than on impulse. He would have been capable of a planned assassination.

is. but everything is normal, right down to June's little fingernails.

I don't think we'll be at this address much longer so it is not advisable for you to visit here.

The reason for the delay in some letters and the speed in others is because of the Russian censor who reads all letters.

I was not aware you sent other letters to me in the Hotel when I lived in moscow and I left there for minsk after I wrote that letter.

I cannot say where we shall go at first probably directly to Vernon.

Love
Al

Although the sample of Sirhan Sirhan's handwriting included here is only his signature, his basic personality traits are revealed clearly. His nature is impulsive and hot-headed, likely at any time to explode into aggressive action. His action in killing Senator Robert F. Kennedy could have followed a build-up of antagonistic feeling that let go uncontrollably.

REVERSE SIDE OF APPLICATION NO. *F.A.523716*

CONFIDENTIAL INFORMATION SEC. 1808 V.C.

(3) Applied for a license under a former or different name.
(4) Had driving privilege or a license cancelled, refused, suspended or revoked.
(5) Held a license in another state within the past 3 years.

N O EXCEPTIONS TO (3), (4) AND (5)

I Hereby Certify, Under Penalty of Perjury, That All Statements on This Application Are True.

18 ℔ Mar. 64 _____ x *Sirhan Sirhan*
(Date)   (Signature of Applicant)

ACCEPTANCE OF LIABILITY BY PARENTS

Pursuant to Sections 17700 through 17706 and in assumption of the liability specified in Sections 17707 through 17710 of the Vehicle Code, the undersigned residents of the State of California join in this application and certify, under penalty of perjury, that all statements made hereon are true and correct.

Father	*Father lives*	Mother	x *Mary Sirhan*
Address	*in Jordan*	Address	*696 E. Howard St.*
City	Date	City *Pasadena*	Date *18 Mar. 64*
Int. Lic.	Date **MAR 20 1964**	Examination has been given as indicated and	
L.P.	Date	approved that license be granted.	
Q.L.	Date	*[signature]*	
(DL22)		Examiner	Badge

The author was asked by a national publication to analyze Sirhan Sirhan's handwriting for a clue to his real character. I described the assassin of Senator Robert Kennedy as: "impetuous, hot-headed and possessing an explosive personality—quick-tempered, inconsistent and unstable; acting on impulse."

This personality analysis was made over six months before the trial of Sirhan Sirhan. Two other graphologists also examined Sirhan's script and we all agreed that Sirhan was filled with inner conflicts that compelled him to act impulsively. None of us knew that other handwriting analysts were being asked to analyze Sirhan's script, and all of us concurred on every detail of the character delineation.

Do you do too much unproductive worrying?

If you have a tendency to do too much unproductive worrying, your handwriting will be small and heavy-pressured, and your capital letters will be simply constructed. Worrying becomes dangerous when you allow your full mental faculties to be concerned with the smallest details of living.

For instance, if you are due an Income Tax refund and you think about it constantly so that it shows in your attitude toward others that you have "something on your mind," then your worrying is classified as unproductive. "Why worry?" is your best advice. You can solve your problem in a few minutes by calling up the Tax Bureau to inquire about your refund. After that your over-concern with the matter will disappear. Your worry was based upon the simple fact (registered in your subconscious mind), that you thought there was nothing you could do about an apparent injustice. As soon as you take some definite course of action your anxiety will be erased.

Everybody worries but it is only dangerous to those persons who could deteriorate into obsessed feelings or states of debilitating depression. Mental illness could result, occasionally leading to suicide. Self-destruction is the end product of a vivid mental compulsion to clear away an unbearable worry or fear.

If, in addition to the graphological signs already mentioned, you extend your capital letters with snail-like rings, partly enclosing the capitals, you are one short step from serious mental illness. When you take the next step you will not be able to think logically and your writing will take an abnormal formation, depending on what type of mental illness you have lapsed into. At this stage someone else will have to classify you!

Carelessness in important matters

Many people are careless about important matters but do not realize this because of their lack of sensitivity to other people and what these other persons consider important. It is not necessary to know exactly what every individual you meet thinks is important, but it is helpful to realize that everyone does not look at life the way you do.

At first thought this point may be so obvious that it hardly merits discussion. This is not so. If you are not aware of what other people feel happy about it is because you are lacking in mental breadth, consciously careless of details, and selfish.

There is little physical danger in sliding over or in omitting important details, but you will miss much of life's delightful subtleties, at least as far as person-to-person activities are concerned, if you look at the world perched on a personal pedestal.

You must put yourself in the other person's shoes and try to think as he would think under the same set of circumstances.

Unfortunately, most people are careless about important matters as they concern others. The greatest offenders, as seen in their handwriting, are those who write with a medium or large hand, use a very heavy pressure, slant their handwriting forward, write almost illegibly, and make their capital letters extremely large and flourished.

Carelessness, as such, is generally characterized by light pressure, plain small letter formations, careless or incorrect punctuation, and badly-spaced lines of writing. Carelessness in itself is not a danger because it can be changed to carefulness through proper training. Disregard for other people's ideas is an overbearing projection of selfishness to the point where it damages the well-being of others.

Recognizing the lazy person

Dreams never come true for lazy people. Laziness is noted in light-pressured writing, small letters which are made slowly and with the small m's and n's rounded at the top, and by plain capital letters. The entire script indicates lack of drive and energy and the small letters are *never* made small but tend toward a large hand. All of the previous signs hold true for the average lazy individual. When the laziness is present in the handwriting of an educated person—some training beyond high school—the pressure becomes medium and the writing takes on a vertical appearance. The other signs remain the same.

Lazy.

Careless.

Summary

As a doctor watches for dangerous changes in blood pressure you can keep personal tabs on your pen pressure to check on your health. You can be your own psychiatrist, mildly speaking, by studying the condition of your mind as reflected in the variations in your handwriting. Whatever your problem may be, you will have the special advantage of looking at yourself objectively since you can see yourself in your script. Dangers will be avoided because you will know about them before they can ruin you. Handwriting information can be compared to knowing the way things will happen before they happen. It is like being sure a head-on auto crash is to occur but because you are forewarned you avoid the collision by steering away from the danger.

So use handwriting power to pull you away from dangerous practices and harmful habits.

Part 4

Making use of the opportunities that handwriting knowledge offers you

13. Determining your own personality qualifications through handwriting

Classify yourself

Following is a collection of *general* personality patterns which will make it easy for you to type yourself quickly by merely glancing at your handwriting.

Only *one* graphological sign is given for each type. If this sign is neutralized by one or more contradictory signs, then you only have *tendencies* in the direction of that kind of personality.

This is only a *general* classification and will hold true only in a general way. Types of more specific detail are listed in the section following.

The reflective type

Thinks rather than acts: small writing.

to analyze the
of the individual.

The active type

Acts rather than thinks: large writing.

have also done
station. This

The natural type

Thinks, acts, and feels normally with no psychological complexes: forward slanting writing.

I am a pu school teacher

The repressed type

Does not give true and free expression to his normal desires for affection: backhand writing.

Classes a and also

The intellectual type

Lives for knowledge rather than feeling and enjoyment: small writing.

information

The feeling type

Lives for feeling and enjoyment rather than knowledge: medium-size writing.

something that she

The egocentric type

Every move he makes is a selfish, self-centered one: unusually tall capitals.

The altruistic type

His actions are chiefly objective, tending to give service to others: long, horizontal finals.

Introduction to Specific Personality Types

Human nature is like the myriads of colored refractions from a sparkling diamond. Like the diamond, it "reacts" only when stimulated. Light is the stimulant in the case of the diamond, but with human nature almost anything may act as a stimulant. A person may be influenced or inhibited toward a certain reaction because of stimuli of temperature, human environment, visual impressions, sensual arousings, and so forth.

Regarding human nature, causes are about the same with most people but the way they react depends upon their past experiences as well as their physical and mental heredity. A person who has been taught how to write will naturally form letters similar to the ones with which his memory attaches concrete significance. But reasonably, also, this person will vary his letter formations according to his individuality, originality, temperament, taste, skill, degree of carefulness, and a hundred other acting influences which directly or indirectly cause his script to be different from the standard letter formations. Psychographology, as previously stated, is based upon this very logical assumption.

In 1492 Columbus went on a voyage of discovery and found land. Later, when most of the land of the world was known and charted, the great advances of exploration in the scientific world began. Invention followed invention. Man is an incessant explorer. Now he has become tired of exploring the material world and is voyaging upon the many uncharted waters of the mental universe. He is venturing into the vastness and complexity of the human mind. Psychology as a science has been well-substantiated, and out of psychology have come psychiatry and psychoanalysis. To these we now add our newest psychological science: *Psychographology.*

Taking the science of psychology and using its terms and methods in relation to Graphology, we get the very useful and practical science of psychographology. By means of graphological indications it is possible for the psychographologist to pick out the various traits of character of an individual. But unless these traits were organized into some sort of pattern they would be like so many designs in a crazy-quilt, a veritable hodge-podge. With the aid of psychology, however, it is possible to build up from these fragments a "behavior pattern" which will serve as a key to the possible and the probable reactions of the individual in question. He can be classified as this or that *type* of person.

Because people, in general, are of such similitude as regards behavior and reactions, when circumstances are parallel and environmental conditions are alike, they are easily classified into psychological types. Modern psychology recognizes the type theory of personality. This section of the book goes a step further and shows how the specific type to which a person belongs can be ascertained by a systematic study of his handwriting.

Perhaps an explanation would clear the atmosphere. We are all acquainted with various kinds of people and, quite naturally, we classify them, perhaps unconsciously, into types. How often do we hear the expressions:

"Oh, he's just a crank."

"Look at that 'publicity hound.' "

"He's a gentleman."

"What a dignified-looking person."

"He's the kind that would bite the hand that fed him."

Each of the quoted statements bears a definite relation to a special kind of person. But is it logical to conclude, since there are certain types, that every human being is a crank, a gentleman, a publicity hound, or one of the numerous other types?

We cannot come to that simple conclusion. The truth of the matter is that most of us are a mixture of two or more types. As our type becomes less distinct and we lose definiteness of action we become "average."

How to classify individuals through handwriting

Admitting that there do exist certain types of individuals, let us see how types are related to Graphology, or rather how handwriting is so indicative of the personality of the writer that we can clearly classify the writer as a certain type of individual.

Suppose we use as an example the handwriting of a very romantic young woman. Most girls are romantic to a certain extent, but this girl is an *erotomaniac*. Her whole existence is built around her love for the opposite sex. She is continually falling in and out of love. She is alternately soaring in the skies and grovelling in the dust. She is very easily pleased and quickly hurt. She can stand physical stress but is overcome by mental strain. In other words, this mentally sick person is a *type*.

Now is it not plausible that a person of her nervous disposition and of her peculiar personality pattern should write a hand consistent with her individuality? It is a known fact that the tension of the nervous system has much to do with the way we write. A very nervous and excitable person writes fast, the letter forms being sharp, indefinite, and in some cases almost cryptic. In contrast to this we notice that the phlegmatic, passive person writes a hand which is distinguished by its definite letter formations, its slow easy rhythm, and its rounded letter forms.

Characteristics of the overly romantic type

The distinguishing characteristics of the script of the abnormally romantic type are:
* *1. A forward-leaning hand.
* *2. More than the usual amount of quotation marks, exclamation points, and so forth.
* *3. Letters larger at the end of each word than at the beginning.
* *4. Irregular base line.
* 5. Bad spacing of lines.
* *6. Average or light pressure of script.
* *7. Exaggerated capital letters with peculiar finals or beginning strokes.
* 8. t-bars to the right or flying off stem.
* *9. Careless punctuation.
* *10. Muddy, hasty appearance of writing.

Unless *all* these signs are found in an individual's handwriting, he is not a *true* type. If one or more of the signs listed under the specific type are missing then a person may be a *monotype,* a *duotype,* or a *complex,* depending upon the number of elements lacking. If one element is lacking, providing it is *not* one of those *starred,* he is a *monotype;* that is to say, a person who is so typical of a class as to be called by its name, though not necessarily being a *true* type. If two elements of *those starred* are absent, he is a *duotype;* in other words, one who probably has a double personality and has two opposing forces that complicate his life. Finally, there is the *complex,* which name is given to all those whose handwriting does not lend itself to clear classification in any particular type, but which is actually a combination of several types.

In the concluding pages of this book will be found a section devoted to a description of a great many types. To try to unsystematically analyze the handwriting of someone and to endeavor to place it in its proper type-classification would entail needless thumbing of pages and tiresome reading of the various signs significant of these special types. Therefore, a very simple system has been arranged by which script can be "keyed out" in a comparatively brief period of time. The key precedes the list of types.

Before using the type section, read the pages devoted to the rudiments of Graphology, not so much to learn what each sign in handwriting means, but more to familiarize yourself with the language of Graphology. Then when you use the key to the types you will understand the technical terminology employed.

Key to the Types

How to use the Key

It is not necessary to begin at the beginning of the key; you may start anywhere. The key is merely an elaborated index and is to be used mainly in the classification of script the nature of which is unknown.

Pick out the one or two distinguishing characteristics of the script. This done, turn to the part of the key which treats of the information found. The writing may be very fancy and replete with flourishes; in that instance turn to Flourishes, listed under General Features. Under "Presence of flourishes" there appear two numbers that refer to the possible types into which a person may fall if he uses flourishes in his writing. Turn to the "Description of Types" section and examine the lists of graphological signs for each type listed, referring first to those types which are *starred.* Remember there are four kinds of type-classifications: *true* type, *monotype, duotype,* or *complex.* True types are rare, as are monotypes; duotypes are common, while complexes predominate.

Summary of the Types

TRUE TYPE All graphological signs present.

MONOTYPE One sign missing but must *not* be one of those *starred.*

DUOTYPE Two signs missing but *must* be those signs *starred.*

COMPLEX Three or more signs missing of those *starred.*

A. General Features

   1. General appearance of writing*

Crowded	Uniform	Diffused
14	14—37—41	9—11
17	42—46	12—13
23—24—43		26

Uneven	Poorly spaced	
12	25—44	31—44
		51

Loop letters clearly separated from lines above and below: 3—6—40—41—48.
Loop letters running into lines above and below: 25—28—31.
Words close together: 27.
Legible: 18.

   2. Style of writing

Conventional	Original	Fixed
26—29	10—15—18	11—29
45	35	

Graceful	Inartistic	
10—18	12	
20—40	23—33	
	37	

Square writing: 3.
Odd or unusual style of writing: 35.
Only one form for each letter: 29.
Adherence to old-fashioned capitalizations: 29.
Refined, pleasing, and interesting letter-forms: 18.
Exclamation points, interrogation marks, quotation marks, and under-score used more often than is generally the case: 47.

  * Refer to the *italicized* type numbers first.

3. General slope of writing

Backhand	Vertical	Forward
1	1—3—6	1—3—6
17—23	7	11—12
36—42	10—13—17	13
	22—23	22
	33	31—32
	35—42	33—39—46
	46	47—51
	48	

Varying slopes in same specimen of writing: 2.

4. Shape of writing

Angular	Round	Mixed
1—3	6—10—12	6
9—11—13	39	
16—17		
22—35		
39—42—44		
46—48		

5. Size of writing

Small	Large	Medium
1—3—5	6—11—12	6—11
9	31—32	12—34
17—18	34	40—41—46
33—35—43	40	51

6. Lines of writing

Well spaced	Poorly spaced	Widely spaced
9—14	22	31—50
15—19	25	
34—40—46		
48—50		

Ascending	Converging
7—9	22

7. The basic line

Straight	Uneven
4—7—11	5
33—37—40	
46—48	

8. Speed of writing

Quick	Slow	Broken Rhythm
9—11	12	8
15		28
18—25		
36—39		
46		

Letters in words occasionally omitted: 8.
Many letters only half-formed: 9.
Words connected with sweeping dashes: 45.

9. Pressure

Heavy	Light	Medium
3—11	6—8—10	1—6—12
16—22—23		31
51	50	39—40
		46—47

Weak Strokes	Coarse Strokes	Steady
12—28	23	3—6—11
32	24—51	33—37—46
36—43		

Initial pressure heavier than following pressure: 27.
Strokes tremulous with slight catches here and there in upper loop letters: 44.
Muddy writing: 23.

10. Shading

Conscious	Natural	Coarse
22	7—11—12	14
Copper-plate	15—21	
33—37	33—37	
41—45—46	41—45—46	

11. Capitals

Simple	Ornate	Proportionate
1—4—6	23	10—11
9—12—15	27	13—26
30—33—46		40

Wide at base	Very high
16	27

(a) Individual capitals

First stroke of capital E inflated: 27.
Incurve on capital H: 29.
Full-bellied P's and R's: 6.

12. Flourishes

Presence of flourishes: 27—47.

13. Margins

Close to edge	Proportionate	Wide
41	10—15	10—31

Left even	Left uneven	None
12	23	14—48

Left margin getting wider as it proceeds down the page: 31.
(Note: If this sign is present in very hasty writing it should be disregarded.)
Left margin decreasing in width as it proceeds down the page: 24.

14. The signature

Dotted with period	Fluently written
12	41

15. Punctuation

Careful	Careless	Absent
3—10	8	8
14—17—24	31—49	
40—41		

16. Ending-strokes of words

Ascending to right	Extending horizontally	Ending with hook
11—39—40	31—46	9—17
46—49		24—45
	Lasso ending on w	Short or clipped
	20	1—38

Ending strokes point straight up: 50.
Ending strokes soar high above words: 12.

(a) Beginning strokes of letters

Incurves on capitals M and R	No incurves	Inflexible
29	13—23	51

B. Special Features

1. Shape of small letters

Pointed at top	Rounded at top	Letters very full, bloated
11—38	6	14
41		

2. Relation of small letters to each other

Connected	Disconnected	Words occasionally omitted
3—10—11	10—20	16
12—16—24	50	
32—45		
48		

3. Size of small letters

Last letter in word larger than first: 12—33—37.
Last letter in word smaller than first: 16—30—36—41.
All letters the same size: 40.

Small letters of varying sizes	Wavy ending strokes	Small letters high
4—5	17—24	40
23		
38		

4. Loops

Long below	Short below	Long above
6—11—12	3	18—20
20—31	Short above	32
39—46	22	Made with stroke
47		3—46

5. Small letters a and o

Open at top	Closed at top
12	1—5—16
32	30—38

6. Small letter b

Incurve present: 32.

7. Small letter d

Looped	Stroke	High stem
6—32	11	12

Final stroke below line: 21—45.
Ending stroke curved upward: 18.

8. Small letter e

Greek form: 10.

9. Small letter f

Looped	Return stroke to right	Return stroke to left
20	20—45—48	29

10. Small letter i—manner of dotting

High above stem	*Close to stem*
15	17

(a) Small letter i—force and kind of dots

Appear like dashes	*Dots omitted*
13—44	8—28

11. Small letters m and n

Like w and u	*Unlike w and u*
26	23

12. Small letter p

Lower loop returns on left of letter: 26.
Lower point sharp, with upstroke on right of stem: 11—13—51.
Small letter s tied to upstroke, or at least closed: 5.

13. Small letter t—manner of crossing

Strongly	*Weakly*	*t-bar above stem*
7—9—11	43	8—13—18
45		20—49—51

t-bar low down on stem	*Evenly or carefully crossed*	*Long and sweeping*
26	6—7	20
	41—46	47

Short	*Uncrossed*	*Pointed upward*
6—16	8—28	7—9—10
		16

Pointed downward	*To right of stem*	*Begins thick, ends thin*
11—45	3—7—11	13
	13—20	
	49—51	

14. Small letter t—the t-stem

Tent-shaped	*Looped*	*Inflated*
22	6—16	14
	32	

Final downstroke below line
21—45

15. Numerals

Numerals 7 and 9 with graceful tails projecting below line: 42.
Numeral 5 made with two separate strokes: 3—42.
Numeral 2 made like a sea-gull: 3—42.

Description of the Types

1. The Introvert

Characteristics

To begin with, there are very few *true* introverts. Most of us are introverted to a certain degree, but only those who conform completely to the following description are the *true-type* introvert:

He likes to be away from the crowd; is not a "socializer." He is very sensitive to personal criticism. Would rather think than play. Takes life too seriously. Cannot adjust himself to other people's personalities. Subjective rather than objective. Cringes before realities; is annoyed that he has to live in such a world as ours.

Graphological signs

1. Angular script.
2. Closed a's and o's.
*3. Vertical or slightly back-hand slant of writing.
4. Medium pressure.
*5. Broken rhythm.
*6. Small writing.
*7. Clipped or short ending strokes.
*8. Simple or print-like capitals.
*9. Signature enclosed in sweeping curve.

2. Moody Person

Characteristics

This individual is a "creature of mood." He is alternately high and low in spirits. His moods are not even consistent for the length of a day. His feelings are very sensitive to harsh environment and are liable to cause him to turn away from the world and brood in silence when he is irritated or displeased. This person knows the greatest joys and the deepest sorrow.

Graphological signs

*1. Variable size of small letters.
*2. Uneven pressure.
*3. Sharply formed capitals.
*4. Much variation in crossing of the t's.
*5. i dots carelessly made.
6. Diffused writing.
*7. Angular hand.

3. Scientific Type

Characteristics

Looks at the world through mechanistic eyes. Is analytical and discerning in everything he does. Can never lose himself in any pleasing activity. Counts the cost too much. With him the important thing is to understand the *workings* of Nature, let the poet worry about its soul. Has no kinship with the dreamer except that he has an imagination that can visualize unrealities. Never takes chances; figures everything out to a logical conclusion before he takes action.

Graphological signs

*1. Small writing.
*2. Definite letter formations, sometimes cryptic.
*3. Heavy, steady pressure.
 4. Careful punctuation.
*5. Figures made sharply, 2 like a seagull.
*6. Angular writing.
*7. Well-spaced lines.
*8. Short lower loops, many times sharply made j, y, f.
 9. t-bar on right of stem.
10. Square writing.

4. Versatile Person

Characteristics

Adaptation is this person's middle name. He can fit into any environment. He can execute many things well. His proficiency lies in things mental rather than in manual dexterity. He has a very likeable and attractive personality. He has executive ability. He can live conveniently and agreeably upon either the highest or lowest levels of life, and he "can take it on the chin" and smile!

Graphological signs

*1. Plain capitals.
*2. Ending strokes concave.
*3. Straight lines.
*4. Variable size of small letters.
*5. Angular writing.
*6. Forward slant to writing.

5. Prevaricator

Characteristics

This person can tell some of the tallest stories, yet many people readily believe him because of the casual manner he uses in relating them. He really doesn't know what he is talking about half the time; that is, he does not realize that he is juggling with the truth. He thinks he is quite important yet is not enthusiastic enough in manner to annoy anyone very much by his superior manners.

Graphological signs

*1. Irregular lines.
*2. Small letters varying in size.
*3. a and o tightly closed.
*4. Small letter s closed or tied to upstroke.

*5. t's crossed high.
*6. Rounded writing.

6. Ideal Housewife

Characteristics

Would rather stay home and get her work done than run around to bridge parties and afternoon teas. Always considerate of her husband's likes and dislikes. Never questions or doubts her husband's explanations. Likes children and does all she can for them. Would never consent to having her children taken care of by a nurse. Generally good at cooking and sewing and does not mind hard work. Keeps her home looking clean and comfortable. Spends wisely.

Graphological signs

*1. Rounded or mixed writing.
*2. Simple capitals.
*3. "Full-bellied" P's and R's.
*4. Full-looped g's; y's; etc.
*5. Vertical or forward-slanted writing.
 6. Short or slightly long t-crossings.

*7. Looped stems on d's and t's.
 8. Steady pressure.
*9. Large, legible writing.
 10. Good spacing.
*11. Slow, steady rhythm.
 12. Fine writing.
*13. Tops of small letters never pointed.

7. Strong-willed Person

Characteristics

This person knows exactly *what* he is going to do and *when* he is going to do it. It is as unusual for him to vacillate as it is for a stone wall to bend in the wind. Has set opinions on most things which can be changed only by fool-proof argument. Has strong likes and dislikes. Is apt to be very popular, if a man; vice versa, if a woman.

Graphological signs

*1. Straight lines of writing.
*2. Ascending lines of writing.
*3. Unconscious shading of down-strokes.
4. Vertical writing.

*5. t-bar carefully and deliberately crossing stem; t-bar pointed upward across stem; t-bar dashed heavily to the right of the stem.
*6. Even, steady pressure.

8. Absent-minded Person

Characteristics

Is apt to forget almost anything. Should never be trusted to mail letters which demand speedy transit. Will find it hard to begin talking again if interrupted, due to lapse of memory. Will unconsciously refer to you as "Charles" when your name is "James." Rarely thinks very much about what he is doing, unless he is trying to solve some difficult problem.

Graphological signs

*1. Careless punctuation.
*2. Broken rhythm.
*3. Letters omitted in words.
*4. Occasional t not crossed.

*5. t-bars above stem.
*6. Undotted i's and j's.
*7. Light or uneven pressure.

9. Go-getter

Characteristics

An essentially American type. Does things with a spirit which will not admit defeat. Gets what he wants because of his fervent enthusiasm which wins all who meet up with him. Always ready with a smile, yet a dangerous smile if you get in his way. Very practical while advancing toward his goal, yet very sympathetic and kind when he is relaxing.

Graphological Signs

*1. Fast rhythm.
2. Good spacing between lines.
*3. Different writing.
*4. Angular writing.
5. Small writing.
*6. Many letters only half-formed.
*7. Simple or print-like capitals.

*8. Strong t-crossings.
*9. Hooks in ending-strokes occasionally.
*10. t-bars and lines of writing ascending.
11. Hasty, distinct writing.

10. Lover of Fine Arts

Characteristics

Sees beauty even in the common things of life. Can look at a surrealist painting and say, "Beautiful!" and really mean it. Appreciative of form, color, and value, both those of man's design and of nature's creation. Finds exquisite joy in all forms of art, does not denounce any.

Graphological signs

*1. Vertical writing.
 2. Round writing.
*3. Print-like or simple, graceful capitals.
*4. Greek e's or d's occasionally.
*5. Originality in formation of small letters.
*6. Balanced, well-proportioned margins.
*7. Breaks in words, letters disconnected.
 8. Square capital M.
*9. Neat writing, never coarse.
*10. Down strokes lightly made.
 11. t-bar crossing ascending.

11. High-pressure Salesman

Characteristics

Appeals to your emotions rather than to your reason. Is quick and fast in his talk. Converses with a sureness which is disarming. Thinks faster than he talks. Acts quickly, leaving a hazy impression. Is bold and unafraid in his actions. Always wears a smile which, although it appears sincere, may not always be so.

Graphological signs

*1. Angular writing.
*2. Sharp-stemmed d's and p's.
*3. Forward writing.
*4. Continuous heavy pressure.
 5. Strong t-crossings, many times to the right of the stem.
*6. 45 degrees downward stroke of t in signature.
 7. Lower loop letters long.
*8. Tops of small letters pointed.
 9. Medium or large writing.
*10. Fixed style.
*11. Capitals never low.
*12. Letters never compressed.
 13. Ending strokes ascending to right.
*14. p made with lower point sharp and upstroke on right of stem.
*15. Lines straight.
*16. Steady pressure.

12. Credulous Person

Characteristics

This person is easily imposed upon and very often taken advantage of because of his belief that all men are honest and well-meaning until proven otherwise. He believes everything he hears or reads. Because of his child-like credulity he is liable to be disappointed in people many times.

Graphological signs

1. Diffused writing (extended letter formation)
2. Slow or average rhythm.
*3. Simple capitals.
*4. Round writing.
*5. Full lower loops on p, g, y, etc.
6. Straight left margin.
7. High d stem.
*8. Capital wide at the base.
9. Ending strokes soar high above word.
*10. a and o open.
*11. Large or medium writing.
12. Inartistic writing.
*13. Increase in size of letters in word.

13. Impetuous Type

Characteristics

Likely to do things in a fit of anger which he will regret later. Does things on the spur of the moment. Will suddenly change his plans and do something entirely different. Impatient at delay. Wants a thing done at its specified time. This person usually marries early in life.

Graphological signs

*1. Absence of beginning strokes (initial strokes.)
*2. Dashes for i dots.
3. Capitals never low.
*4. Angular hand.
*5. Vertical or forward writing.
*6. t-bar higher than top of stem, and to the right.
*7. Letters extended, never compressed.
*8. p made with lower point sharp and with the upstroke on the right.
*9. t-bar begins heavy, ends thin.

14. Thrifty Person

Characteristics

We all admire the Scotch for their thriftiness; we should then try to emulate this person because he has made saving an essential part of his life plan. It is as natural for him to save a part of his income each week as it is for water to run down a slope. It does not mean any denial upon his part because he saves what he can reasonably spare. He makes the best use of his money and wastes none on extravagances. His code is: "Spend, but spend wisely."

Graphological signs

*1. Letters close together.
*2. No margins.
*3. Punctuation carefully placed.

*4. Neat, uniform writing.
*5. Vertical writing.
*6. Small letters all the same size.

15. Constructive Type

Characteristics

Thinks in outlines rather than in consecutive single ideas. Likes to put things together, be they words in a crossword puzzle or wheels in a watch. Can see in his mind a finished house even though all you can see is a complicated blueprint. Relates the present to the past. Knows just what will go well together. Appallingly accurate.

Graphological signs

*1. Simple, graceful, print-like capitals.
*2. Neat margins.
*3. Well-spaced lines.
 4. t crossed above the stem.
 5. i's dotted high.

*6. Original letter formations and connections.
 7. Legible signature.
*8. Style odd and unusual.
*9. Cross strokes shaded.
10. Square writing occasionally.

16. Argumentative Type

Characteristics

Never more at home than when winning out in a heated argument. Very logical and analytical in his reasoning. Will correct you on all possible occasions, many times when it isn't really necessary. Talks well, but writes better. Usually not very original. Extremely jealous but does not always reveal that fact.

Graphological signs

*1. Connected letters.
*2. Words occasionally connected.
*3. t-stem looped.
*4. t-bar ascending.

 5. Closed a and o.
*6. Heavy pressure.
*7. Angular writing.
 8. Words tapering.

17. The Miser

Characteristics

No one should need an elaborate description of this person. He is, in mind, just a child. He has not grown out of the habit of hoarding things, such a common trait in children. Hoarding means denial; denial means justification for it. His justification comes in the pleasure he gets from accumulated wealth. But it is a mean pleasure, at that!

Graphological signs

*1. Vertical writing.
*2. Careful punctuation.
*3. Hooks at end of strokes.

*4. Compressed letters.
*5. Final letters hardly finished.
*6. Very small writing.

18. Intellectual

Characteristics

Very apt to be conceited, or at least to have a very healthy self-esteem. Will surprise you at the amount of things he knows. Has an answer to every question. When conversing he sounds artificial and stilted. Usually quite original, but not very clever. Has a good appreciation of the finer things of life.

Graphological signs

*1. Marked prevalence of upper projections.
*2. Harmonious proportions in the writing.
*3. Fast rhythm.

*4. Refined, cultured, pleasing and original character.
5. Easy legibility.
*6. Small writing.
*7. d-final curved upward.

19. The Orator

Characteristics

Original in thought. The possessor of a sharp sense of humor. Emotional in appeal. Likes to see what he can do with his audience. Usually can talk longer than he expected to. Self-confident in bearing but not always pleasingly attired.

Graphological signs

*1. Good spacing between words and lines.
*2. Letters extended.
*3. Connected letters.
*4. Small letters varying in size.

*5. Forward slant.
*6. Long upper loops.
7. Hasty writing.
*8. Open a's and o's.

20. Poet

Characteristics

Very easily hurt, especially by careless remarks. Noise is the very bane of his existence. Would rather walk miles to get away from the noises of the city than to stay at home and endure it. Can write poetry only when "in the mood." Apt to be very impractical in his business dealings. Usually good at sharp repartee. More at home alone or with a very close friend than with a noisy, carefree crowd.

Graphological signs

*1. Charming and graceful writing.
*2. Upper strokes long.
*3. t-bar above stem and to the right.
*4. t-bar sometimes long, sometimes short, now and then a mere dot.

*5. Disconnected letters.
*6. Long f loops.
*7. w rounded, emphasized by a lasso stroke.
8. Long lower loops.
*9. High d stem.

21. Wilful Type

Characteristics

The one thing this person desires is to have his own way. In this desire of his he is, of course, childish. Stubbornness and moodiness go right along with wilfulness. This person is very persistent in his beliefs and will often stick to a point even if it isn't right, just so that folks couldn't say that he was a "quitter."

Graphological signs

1. Unconscious shading.
*2. Final stroke of small letters d and t below line.
*3. Heavy pressure.

*4. Heavy, downward pointing t-bars.
*5. Forward slant.
6. Round i dots.

22. Politician

Characteristics

This person is one of the less desirable of the types. He only looks out for his own good and is ever ready to fleece the public out of what it trusts to his keeping. He gets what he wants, honestly or dishonestly, because he can pull the necessary strings. He is usually very crafty, clever, and diplomatic.

Graphological signs

*1. Energetic writing.
*2. Converging lines.
*3. Shaded writing. (Conscious)
4. Bad spacing.
*5. Angular hand.

*6. Low upper projections on h, k, l.
*7. t's made tent-like.
8. Vertical or slight slant to writing.

23. The Brute

Characteristics

This person will never become refined regardless of the amount of training he might receive. He is of a brutally coarse nature and is endowed with very little common sense. All he can see is his own needs. He will not tolerate interference with his own plans and is like a cornered beast when disturbed. His wants are merely the satisfaction of his physical needs. He has no ambition because he does not have the mind to visualize any greater happiness than eating, drinking, and sleeping.

Graphological signs

*1. Backhand or vertical writing.
2. Constant variation in size of small letters.
*3. Muddy downstrokes.
*4. Coarse, ungraceful style.
*5. No incurves.

*6. Letters never extended.
*7. Ungraceful capitals.
8. n and m unlike w and u.
*9. Heavy cross strokes.
*10. Uneven left margin.

24. Stingy Person

Characteristics

It is quite characteristic for this person to be very stingy to others and yet quite generous to himself. He feels no fine feeling of benevolence at Christmastide, rather does he experience a pang when he recollects what it will cost him in gifts which he just cannot refrain from giving. When he does give there is always a string attached to the gift. He "casts his bread upon water," hoping for an ample return.

Graphological signs

*1. Letters crowded together.
*2. Last letter barely finished.
*3. Hooks at end of strokes.

*4. If in a cultured hand, the punctuation is carefully placed; if in a large hand the strokes are coarse; if in a small hand the strokes are fine.
*5. Vertical writing.
*6. Small letters all the same size.

25. Speculator

Characteristics

This refers to the person who thinks that life is a gamble. He is willing to stake his last dollar on a good chance to win "big money." His type will buy stock on the margin, rather than outright. He will finance new inventions and new ideas. His nature is impatient; he cannot be content with small profits; he must win quickly, whether it be a small amount or a large amount.

Graphological signs

*1. Badly spaced writing.
*2. Lower loop letters extend into line below.
*3. Hasty writing.

*4. t-bar heavy at beginning, thin at end.
*5. Forward slant to writing.
6. Variable size of small letters.

26. Extrovert

Characteristics

This person is the extreme type of extrovert. He is always going somewhere. He cannot see how people can spend quiet evenings at home reading books. Likes to talk but is never really very penetrating in his conversation. Attaches the greatest importance to pleasure.

Graphological signs

*1. Small letters m and n like w and u.
*2. Letters extended.
*3. Capitals not too high.
*4. Downstrokes of p rounding to the left rather than pointed to the right.

*5. t-bar low down on stem.
*6. Style not eccentric.
7. Diffused writing.
*8. Forward slant.

27. Egotist

Characteristics

Thinks of everything in relation to himself. Self-centered but not necessarily selfish. He is most likely to succeed because he has the ability to shut out all interests which tend to sidetrack him from his desired goal. An interesting person to talk with because of his frankness. A very mean person when uneducated; a very likeable person when educated. Education seems to smooth out his roughness.

Graphological signs

1. Words close together.
*2. Initial pressure heavier than the following pressure.
*3. First stroke of capital letter E inflated.

*4. Flourishes.
*5. Capitals too high for body of writing.
6. Elaboration of capitals.
*7. Hasty writing.

28. "Muddlehead"

Characteristics

Likely as not this person is immature in his development. He is what the type-name indicates, very confused in his ideas. He would be impractical in business because his reasoning is illogical and erratic. His sense of proportion is poor as is also his ability to see ahead. He gets general impressions almost exclusively, and for that reason makes many mistakes, mistakes which would not have been made if only a little fine discernment had been his to use.

Graphological signs

*1. Poorly-spaced writing.
*2. Strokes and loops of one line entangled and running into lines above and below.
*3. Letters t and i frequently uncrossed or undotted.

*4. Final letter to words sometimes omitted.
5. Forward slant to writing.
*6. Variable size of small letters.
*7. Uneven pressure.

29. Conservative

Characteristics

This is probably the type of person who invented "red tape." He must know all the "ins and outs" of a situation before he will take action. When buying something, he does not do so on the spur of the moment. He invests rather than speculates. He is slow but sure. He never makes any lucky "hits" because he doesn't take any long chances.

Graphological signs

*1. Fixed style of writing.
*2. Only one form used for each letter.
*3. Lack of originality in letters or writing.

*4. Adherence to old-fashioned style of capitalization and letter forms.
*5. Unnecessary beginning strokes as for example, the incurves on capitals H and K.

30. Diplomat

Characteristics

This individual always seems to be able to get himself out of any mix-up regardless of its seriousness. He is adept at stopping arguments and in bringing order out of chaos. He knows when to refrain from saying too much. He never becomes "involved." He says the right thing at the right time in the right place.

Graphological signs

*1. Letters in words diminishing in size.
*2. First small letter of word larger than the rest.
*3. Plain capitals.

*4. a and o closed.
*5. Forward slant to writing.
*6. Angular writing.

31. Spendthrift

Characteristics

This person is not only careless of the way in which he spends his money but also of what he says and does. He often misjudges, miscalculates, and misunderstands. This person can't save money because he has never really tried. He likes to gamble and takes long chances. But he enjoys life more than most people.

Graphological signs

*1. Diffused hand.
*2. Letters and words widely spaced.
*3. Margins wide.
*4. Margin getting wider toward bottom.

5. Usually in large writing.
*6. Ending strokes long and horizontal.
*7. Lower loop letters run into the lines below.

32. The Chatterbox

Characteristics

The incessant talking of this individual concerning trivial matters is very irritating sometimes. Thinks something is wrong if there is a "lull" in the conversation. Usually fairly credulous. Not a very deep reasoner. Can usually talk more intelligently on TV stars than on psychology.

Graphological signs

*1. Upper strokes very long.
*2. t and d with wide inflated loops.
*3. a and o open.
*4. b with initial short "tick" at beginning of letter.

*5. Weak strokes.
6. Forward slant to writing.
*7. Large writing.

33. Sincere Person

Characteristics

This person is natural and unaffected in speech and manners. He speaks frankly and directly. He is sincere in all he does and finds no pleasure or profit in telling lies. His life is stainless of crime. He is very apt to be imposed upon by unscrupulous persons. He is very credulous. He gives most people the benefit of the doubt.

Graphological signs

*1. Straight lines.
*2. Small letters equal size.
*3. Inartistic, schoolboy hand, or the tendency to ungraceful writing.

*4. Letters increase in size in the words.
*5. a's and o's open at top.
*6. Forward slant.

34. Broad-minded Person

Characteristics

It is a real pleasure to converse with this person because no matter what you say he will always listen to you with an open mind. He is always willing to be shown wherein he might be wrong. He sees and appreciates life's fullest values. He believes that everyone who wants a chance should be given one. Always considerate, kind, and helpful.

Graphological signs

*1. Words well-spaced.
*2. Medium or large writing.
*3. t's crossed high, many above stem.

*4. d and t made with loops.
*5. a's and o's open at top.
*6. Forward slope to writing.
*7. Variable size of small letters.

35. Inventor

Characteristics

This type refers to the kind of person Edison would be representative of, one who has the ability to make new and better things by a unique combination of the old. He is as much a designer as a constructor. This person sees possibilities for improvement in everything. He believes almost anything is possible. He has great vision and foresight.

Graphological signs

*1. Original method of making connections of letters and words.
*2. Even pressure.
*3. Square writing.

*4. Odd or unusual style of writing.
*5. Definite round i dots.
*6. Small or average sized writing.
 7. Angular writing.
*8. Vertical hand.

36. Deceitful Person

Characteristics

Many of us are diplomatic because we really have to be, but that isn't deceit. Deceit is wilful and malicious misrepresentation. A person of the deceitful type will at any time lie his way out of a "ticklish" situation, using one lie to cover another, regardless of how serious his deception might be. He is the kind who, after you trust him with important business secrets, will sell them to competitors of yours for a consideration.

Graphological signs

*1. Backhand writing.
*2. Decreasing size of letters in words.
*3. Fast writing.

*4. Weak strokes.
 5. Angular hand.
*6. Low stems on small d's.

37. Honest Person

Characteristics

Honesty will always remain the best policy with this person because from his childhood up he has been a model of integrity. Honesty with him is a habit. He is usually frank and outspoken. He does not believe in hiding behind a false front. If he were to serve on a jury he would be sure to render a fair decision.

Graphological signs

*1. Straight base lines.
*2. Inartistic writing.
*3. Last letter in word larger than first.
*4. Increasing size of letters in words.

*5. Uniform writing.
*6. Small letters all the same size.
*7. Steady pressure.

38. Dishonest Person

Characteristics

Most people would find it difficult to associate this person with corruption. He believes in presenting a false front. He realizes he is dishonest and endeavors to cloak his corruption by pretending to be strictly honest. He is quite clever and is rarely caught napping. Usually is honest in a *few* things.

Graphological signs

*1. Small letters a and o tightly closed.
2. Irregular lines.
*3. Base line wavy.

*4. Small letters constantly changing in size.
*5. Small letters pointed at top.
*6. Ending strokes never ascending to the right.

39. Affectionate Type

Characteristics

This person is fully appreciative of the part sex plays in life and is willing to let it have its logical sway. Persons of this type succeed very well as husbands and wives.

Graphological signs

*1. Right slope to writing.
*2. Long lower loops.
*3. Rounded or angular writing.

*4. Long ending strokes turning up to the right.
*5. Fast rhythm.
*6. Variable size of small letters.

40. Big-hearted Type

Characteristics

Always likes to be doing something for somebody and usually does. He is the kind who gladdens the hearts of bell-hops with dollar tips. When in a position to be so, he is very philanthropic. This person is the joy of wives who are pleasure-seekers because he gives them whatever they desire, without asking too many questions. He is never selfish or self-centered.

Graphological signs

*1. Small letters made high.
2. Downstrokes concave.
*3. Words and lines well-spaced.
*4. Every letter carefully made.
*5. Capitals never low.
*6. Style never coarse or ungraceful.
*7. Lines straight.
*8. Small letters equal size.

41. Manager

Characteristics

Highly capable of handling all types of personalities. Can teach others what he would like them to know. Able to discriminate between workers and non-workers. Tactful in his remarks, definite and sure in his actions. Never loses control of himself. Always willing to listen to reason. Democratic in bearing. Makes friends easily. Can inspire others with his own enthusiasm.

Graphological signs

*1. Small letters neither very low nor very high.
*2. Strokes and loops of one line clearly separated from lines above and below.
*3. Small letters pointed at top.
*4. Punctuation carefully made.
*5. Margins never wide.
*6 t carefully crossed.
*7. Letters not widely spaced.
*8. Small letters decreasing in size.
9. Unconscious heavy shading.
10. Signature fluently written.

42. "Mathematical" Mind

Characteristics

Quick and accurate at figures. Practical and efficient in business matters. Logical reasoner. Can solve cryptograms and decipher codes. Quite boring, however, as a conversationalist because of his purely materialistic ideas upon cultural subjects. Never marries early.

Graphological signs

*1. Vertical or backhand writing.
*2. Angular writing.
*3. Figures well and gracefully formed.
*4. Numerals 7 and 9 with final strokes ending gracefully below the line.

*5. 5 made with two separate strokes.
*6. 2 made like a seagull.
*7. All attempt at ornamentation of figures absent.
*8. Careful and precise style of writing.

43. Narrow-minded Person

Characteristics

The characteristics of this person are plainly evident. He tries to judge everybody by himself and since he is selfish, inconsiderate, and lacking in sociability he thinks everyone else is. His judgment is poor because he only sees the obvious things; he cannot weigh both sides of a question. He is certain that what he believes is true. This person is very hard to get along with.

Graphological signs

*1. Small writing.
*2. Words close together.
*3. t-crossings weak.

*4. Crowded spacing.
*5. Simple capitals.
*6. Ending strokes point downward and to the right.

44. Nervous Type

Characteristics

It is a sad thing for the people of this type who must live in "cities of dreadful noises." Every little rattle, crack, bang, or smash disturbs them as much as would a slap in the face. They are troubled with insomnia, have very sick headaches, become depressed very easily, and find much of life rather boring.

Graphological signs

*1. Angular writing.
*2. Strokes tremulous, slight catches here and there, observed more generally in the lower and upper loop letters.

*3. Slurred letter formations.
*4. Dash-like i dotting.
*5. Uneven pressure.
*6. Variable size of small letters.

45. Opinionated Person

Characteristics

It is very hard to get along with this person because he has such strong faith in the correctness of his own ideas. He is adamant in the face of convincing argument. He will stand by his guns even when he knows that he is mistaken. It is useless to argue with this type of person because he will rarely admit that he is wrong. When he does admit he is mistaken, he endeavors to "explain" his way out.

Graphological signs

*1. Words connected with sweeping dashes.
*2. Unconscious shading of downstrokes.
*3. Small letters f made with stroke instead of loop.
*4. t heavily crossed; usually pointing downward.
*5. Finals end with hook and point downward.
*6. Conventional writing.
*7. Letters connected, sometimes words.
*8. t-bar crossed downward, snappishly.
*9. Final strokes of small letters d and t below the line.
*10. Hooks on ending strokes.

46. Organizer

Characteristics

He has an innate ability to see everything in its proper relationship. He can coordinate seemingly unlike factors or personalities so that they will function efficiently and systematically. He has an unlimited capacity for work, chiefly along mental lines. Very broadminded, quite considerate, and always appreciative of favors done for him.

Graphological signs

*1. Vertical or forward slant to writing.
*2. Hasty, uniform writing.
*3. Lines well-spaced.
*4. Plain capitals.
*5. Lower loop letters finish with stroke, or long loop.
*6. Angular writing.
*7. Ending strokes turn up to right.
*8. Even t-crossing.

47. Romantic Type

Characteristics

Quite the person to have at a party because he is very capable of acting silly. Can forget himself and can lose himself in the spirit of a crowd. Is very much extroverted. Likes to talk about love, women, and so forth. Demonstrative when it comes to love-making. Believes that a romantic environment is half the battle in courtship. A great believer in himself.

Graphological signs

*1. Flourishes.
*2. Exclamation points and under-scores much used.
3. Long loops.

*4. Forward slope.
*5. Long t-crossings.
*6. Fast rhythm.

48. Practical Type

Characteristics

This person leads a very materialistic life. He is always figuring out the cost of things. His idol is money. He worships the "Almighty Dollar." He can usually get what he wants because he is able and willing to pay for it. He would rather that a public park be subdivided into lots and sold to individuals for business development than have it remain a playground for children. Being practical in everyday matters is his religion.

Graphological signs

*1. Exact punctuation.
*2. Words and lines well-spaced.
*3. Legible and neat writing.
4. Average-size writing.
*5. Margins absent.

*6. Vertical writing.
*7. Angular hand.
8. Straight lines.
*9. Connected letters.
*10. Small letter f made with stroke instead of loop.

49. Excitable Type

Characteristics

It is wise not to try to repress this type because he flares up very easily. But like a house afire, he is soon out. He is sensitive to what other people say. Easily stirred into activity; easily urged to do right or wrong. One can play upon this person's emotions. Easily frightened, loses his head in a panic.

Graphological signs

*1. t-bar dashed off to right of, and above, stem.
*2. Ending strokes ascending to the right.
*3. Punctuation carelessly done.

*4. Variable size of small letters.
 5. Forward slope to writing.
*6. a's and o's open at top.

50. Psychic Individual

Characteristics

This type is not come upon very often, but those belonging to it have easily recognizable characteristics. They have a far away, dreamy look in their eyes. They are nervous and full of inhibitions. They love the night and the stars as the coal-miner loves the sunlight. They can see "beyond." Life means more than just living physically, their real life centers in the metaphysical. They receive comfort, courage, and inspiration from the unseen world of the spirit. They fascinate you by their piercing gaze; they thrill you by solemn intonations of their speaking; they mystify you by the strangeness and wistfulness of their ideas.

Graphological signs

*1. Disconnected letters, the more the letters are separated the greater the significance.
*2. Fine writing.

 3. Well-spaced writing.
*4. Lines widely spaced.
*5. Ending strokes pointing straight up.
*6. Odd capitals.

51. Pugnacious Type

Characteristics

Always seems to be looking for an argument. Would rather contend with someone than do anything else. Will take the opposite side of a question, just to start an argument. Will seldom give in. Doesn't know when he is beaten. Coarse in manners, careless in language, courageous physically, yet apt to be a moral coward.

Graphological signs

*1. Heavy, coarse writing.
*2. Letters begin with a straight inflexible stroke.
*3. Letters never compressed.

*4. t-bar at right of and above stem.
*5. p made with lower point sharp and with upstroke at right of stem.
*6. Forward slant to writing.

14. Now it's up to you!

Getting a new personality

Now that you have found from your handwriting study just what kind of an individual you are, you will want to build a new and better personality. Your job is to change from your present self to the self you want to be.

If you will study your handwriting from day to day as you strive to alter your personality pattern you will see your handwriting change to conform to your new personality. It will be like planting wheat seeds in clods of soil and later seeing a field of golden grain. You will be experiencing the satisfaction that comes from purposeful and happy achievement.

Build on your best traits

Select your strong points to build upon. Find out what your special gifts or talents are, and make the most of them. You need not fear failure now because your handwriting has told you for certain that you *do* have a number of inborn aptitudes that will guarantee you success if you cultivate them.

Weed out your weaknesses

Your next step is to eliminate your weaknesses or at least tone them down to a place of insignificance. It will be fascinating to watch bad habits disappear as you exert effort to erase them. You will know when they are gone because your writing will mirror the formation of the good habits which you will form to replace the bad ways of doing things.

An example of a fault possessed by many people, and one you will be able to spot quickly and work to remove, is the *negative* outlook. Switch to constructive thinking by taking the positive approach.

Enjoy the easy art of getting along with people

Now that you are beginning to understand yourself better and getting a behind-the-scenes picture of what other people are like, you will find it easier to work with other people, and they will enjoy working with you. The necessity of getting along with other people, since it is they as much as you who determine your failure or success, is important in happy living.

The skill of getting along with others cannot be acquired simply by reading about it. You must practice the principles involved in pleasing people. Study your writing to see which of these harmonizing attitudes you lack, and then do something about changing your character so as to include them in your new *you*.

1. Thoughtful—the art of helping other people get what they want.
2. Understanding—seeing the other person's viewpoint and being sympathetic with it.
3. Pleasant—the assumption that no one is trying to harm you, hence you have no room in your heart for unpleasantness.
4. Cooperative—going along with an existing situation rather than bucking it even when you think you are perfectly justified in not cooperating.

Start being an individual

Stop imitating isolated good characteristics that you notice in others every so often and be the unique individual that you can be by building on the undeveloped pattern of personality that only you possess. There is no other person in the world just like you, so start changing yourself today. Now you have the power to do it. You have discovered yourself in your handwriting.

Finally

No matter how much you discover about yourself, and regardless of how clever you become in understanding other people, you will never achieve your best unless you look beyond yourself for spiritual guidance and power.

As the Right Reverend Cuthbert Bardsley, Bishop of Croydon, England, always said when he was confronted with tasks that seemed impossible to accomplish, "With God's help, I can do it."

I know. That is how this book was written.

INDEX